Claire Miller

Y0-ELJ-265

THE FURNITURE BUYER'S HANDBOOK

THE FURNITURE BUYER'S HANDBOOK

How to Buy, Arrange, Maintain and Repair Furniture

MAX and CHARLOTTE ALTH

WALKER AND COMPANY New York

ACKNOWLEDGMENTS

The author wishes to thank the following for permission to use the illustrations on the pages indicated:

Armstrong Flooring, page 51; Cabin Crafts, page 30; Flexsteel Industries, pages 21 top, 22, 86, 89, 90, 96; Henredon Furniture Company, pages 82, 83 top, 98, 99, 102, 109, 118; Hickory Manufacturing Company, pages 59, 106; The Hitchcock Chair Company, pages 60, 61; Karastan Carpets, pages 23, 103; Kroehler Manufacturing Company, pages 15, 21 bottom; Lees Carpets, page 104; Selig, Inc., pages 83 bottom, 119.

Copyright © 1980 by *Max Alth*

All rights reserved. No part of this book may
be reproduced or transmitted in any form or by
any means, electric or mechanical, including
photocopying, recording, or by any information
storage and retrieval system, without permission
in writing from the Publisher.

First published in the United States of America
in 1980 by the Walker Publishing Company, Inc.

Published simultaneously in Canada by Beaverbooks,
Limited, Pickering, Ontario.

ISBN: 0-8027-0636-3 (cloth)
      0-8027-7155-6 (paperback)

Library of Congress Catalog Card Number: 79-64815

Printed in the United States of America

10 9 8 7 6 5 4 3 2 1

Book designed by Lena Fong Hor

Dedicated to

> *Sy*
>
> *Misch*
>
> *Mike*
>
> *Mendel and*
>
> *Arabella without whose help our furniture would remain soil free and last forever.*

CONTENTS

commission shops; thrift shops; garage sales; house wreckers, salvage yards; newspaper ads; scavenging • Whom can you trust? • Money is not the measure: there is a median range for most items • Beware the rip-off ads: phony sales • Other sales tricks: switch • Sets, suites, and groups • What not to buy: stay away from fads • Finding bargains • Avoiding problems: hold on to your options • Treasure the honest dealer • Interior designers: store designers; free lance designers; services rendered; how do you find a good one? • Delivery

Basic precautions: use reasonable care; tables are not repositories; always use trivets; watch the plates and dishes you put on a bare table; keep all wood surfaces waxed; wipe up all spills immediately; keep all unused upholstery covered; arm guards help; coasters are a must on rugs; deck the furniture with ashtrays; look behind the pillows; vacuum the upholstery; applying soil-proofing compounds; block the sunlight; move your furniture about; watch that moisture • Cleaning tips: polishing requires care; use a clean dust cloth; vacuuming helps; wash spills on wood; attend to soils and stains immediately; accumulated wax; soil in crevices; insect infestation • Spot and stain removal tips: work fast; a towel for liquids; never rub; butter knife for goo and solids; determine the nature of the spill; oil spill; oily residue; water-solvent spills; stains

Surface damage, clear-finish furniture: many very fine scratches; small scratches; deep scratches • Surface damage on painted furniture: burns, scratches; very deep scratches and gouges • Dents and blisters • Loose veneer: loose edges; loose and raised central areas • Missing veneer • Loose legs: on tables; on chairs • Loose wood joints, general • Drawer problems: drawer sticks; drawer too low; drawer comes apart; loose knob • Warped table leaves • Sunken upholstered seats • Replacing padding covers • Replacing caned chair seats and backs • Reweaving rush and other woven seatings

Foreword

Though few of us realize it, furniture is the second largest single investment most of us make in our lifetime. The house, if we are fortunate enough to be able to purchase one, is first. Furniture is second. A car is third. Even if you have no more than an apartment to furnish, the total sum most of us spend on its furnishings will easily exceed the cost of a medium-priced car.

It therefore behooves us to select and purchase wisely and carefully. For no matter what the advertisements say about style and vogue—and the ads always have something different to say every few months—furniture should be for always. There is no such thing as fashions in furniture. What looks good today in your home will look equally good one hundred years from today. Would you, for example say that a piece by Chippendale is dated or old fashioned? Good furniture, moderately well cared for and protected, can last for centuries.

Unfortunately many furniture buyers sink in the morass of technical terms and glib advertising patter. They do not begin to understand what goes into the making of furniture; what the standard sizes are, what the terms mean, what materials are used and which materials are best suited to various purposes.

As a result, many buyers select furniture on the basis of initial cost, advertisements, what the salesman advises and/or what looks good in the showroom, forgetting that the showroom is not their home.

The consequences are often disastrous. Often the furniture does not look attractive or even as though it belongs in the room. It doesn't fit or serve its function well. Worst of all it often falls apart or becomes impossibly soiled in just a few years. And no furniture is so low priced that it can economically be replaced every two or three years.

At the same time many fine pieces of furniture are being discarded today simply because people believe that only old craftsmen, trained since childhood, can properly repair furniture. This, of course, is not so. While some repairs are difficult, many are simple, and much touching up and refinishing can be accomplished beautifully by beginners. With the expenditure of a relatively few dollars and some hours of effort, pieces that might have been thrown out can be made beautiful and useful once again.

This book has been written to provide the knowledge you need when you plan to buy furniture. It explains the various materials and how they are fashioned into furniture; the various sizes, finishes, woods, fabrics, etc., and where and how to find and recognize furniture bargains. Directions for the care and repair of furniture are also included.

In short, this book has been planned to make you a furniture expert, and so enable you to gain the most satisfaction and durability for your money and effort.

M. & C. Alth

1

Develop a Plan

Although the purchase of furniture is simple enough, selecting it is far from simple. There is a tremendous range of styles, designs, materials, sizes, finishes and prices to choose from, more than ever before in history. We all have the same main purposes, even if their order of importance varies from one person to another.

We want

The best furniture possible for our money.

Maximum longevity with minimum maintenance.

Maximum utility and comfort.

The most beautiful furniture possible.

Furniture that reflects our good taste.

Secondary needs will, of course, vary with the individual and his or her situation. These may include:

Child safety.

Easily transported furniture.

Easily saleable furniture.

Furniture with special dimensions.

Furniture with special features.

THE MOST FOR YOUR MONEY

There are three ways of getting a lot of furniture for a little money. You may inherit a houseful of furniture, make your own (this is not as farfetched as it may sound), or you can learn enough about furniture to be able to differentiate between the shoddy, the fair, the good, and the excellent and expend the time and energy necessary to find the best buys.

This book has been prepared with this in mind. The information provided will enable you to evaluate the furniture and rugs you are inspecting intelligently. Price and quality vary greatly between manufacturers, and we believe you will be well rewarded for whatever time you spend looking before you buy.

GROUND RULES

"Shoddy," which during the Civil War meant blankets and clothing that came apart when wet, is no bargain at any price. It is better to eat on fruit crates, if you have to, rather than waste your hard-earned money on a shoddy product.

If you can't find what you want and need, don't compromise. Wait a while and look some more.

One good piece of furniture is better than a number of cheap pieces.

It isn't necessary that a room be filled with furniture, or that it have rugs and floor lamps, etc.

There is no such thing as "modern" style in furniture. Buy what you like, not what a salesman or your friends tell you. You are going to have to live with it.

A good used piece of furniture is always better than a brand-new but cheap piece.

Keep your expenditures in line with your home. A hundred thousand dollars worth of furniture in a twenty-thousand-dollar house looks as bad as, or worse than, a few thousand dollars worth of furniture in a hundred-thousand-dollar house.

Bear in mind that furniture should be for always, so take your time, select, and purchase carefully.

FINANCIAL PLAN

Decide how much you want to spend or how much you can afford to spend for each room you are going to furnish. If you are going to borrow, remember the interest charges, which can amount to an additional $161.72 on a $1,000 three-year loan.

Then look at ads and get approximate costs of each item. Break your total amount down into sums for the individual pieces.

Let us say you are planning to furnish a bedroom and are allotting $1,000. You may decide you want a bed, a dresser, and a single chair. The breakdown might be $600 for the bed, $350 for the dresser, and the remaining $50 for the chair.

Knowing in advance what we should spend will keep us from going astray or being pushed astray by a glib sales clerk. If you are foolish enough to buy more than you can pay for, you will hate whatever you purchase.

The financial road map will also help you keep the level of your purchases steady from piece to piece and room to room. You won't have a magnificent dining room table with two-dollar chairs around it because you spent all your money on the table. The plan keeps you from buying piecemeal and running out of money—or going into hock, which is even worse—in the middle of your furniture buying. This is what happens too often to people without a financial plan. "Only a little more" soon becomes lots more.

PHYSICAL PLAN

Decide what you need in the way of pieces; their size and number. You will need to study the following chapters to secure all the data; this is a must.

For example, suppose you would like to have a dining room table that can seat six. Is your dining room large enough for a table this size, plus chairs, plus the space necessary for diners to rise and get clear of their chair and the table?

If you can comfortably seat six, will there also be room for a sideboard, serving table, flower stand, china closet, or whatever? These considerations are vital. Once your furniture is delivered, it is all yours, and rarely returnable.

On the other hand, perhaps you can seat six by using a narrow dining room table. Chairs without side arms may enable you to seat six comfortably in your dining room. And then again, six may be impossible unless two hold two others on their laps.

The only way to know for certain is to find out the dimensions of the furniture and using chalk, outline the pieces on your floor, leaving space for moving around.

The same holds true for all the rooms. You have to measure them, lay out the planned purchases with chalk or newspaper and see how they will fit.

Delivery. One difficulty, rarely foreseen, may arise when the furniture is brought into the house or apartment. The trouble is not always caused by the size of the doorway. Very often there are sharp turns to negotiate, or curved or angled stairways. Sometimes there is a long narrow hallway that ends in a right-angle turn. Any of these can make it impossible to complete the delivery. The alternative is usually financially very painful.

One alternative is to disassemble the furniture. Piano legs can be removed, or the mirror can be taken off a dressing table. Some of the antique rolltop desks are held together by wood screws and are readily disassembled and put together again.

Another alternative is to bring the piece in through a window. This is a reasonable course if the furniture can go into a first-floor window; but when the piece has to go to an apartment on the 26th floor, you can easily imagine how high the costs of delivery will go.

If you are uncertain about whether or not a particular piece of furniture can be brought into your home and deposited in the proper place, take the hour or two necessary and make a same-size dummy of it by taping cardboard boxes together. Then try the dummy piece of furniture to see how it will go.

If you are purchasing an expensive piece of furniture and delivery is part of the sale, specify that you will only pay when the furniture has been safely deposited at its correct location within your home, and not before. Make the seller worry about whether or not he can get it into your home.

PLAN THE PURCHASE OF EACH PIECE

Furniture has to serve a function in your home. If you don't make certain the furniture you are buying will serve its purpose before you buy it, you may be sorry afterwards. On the other hand, if you buy more furniture than you need, you are wasting money and probably robbing yourself of floor space that is better utilized for other things.

For example, why purchase a dining room table that can seat eight, with eight chairs, if you are a family of four and will almost never need eight places? To take care of the rare guests you might consider a four-person table that expands to seat six, and then keep a card table in a closet. A bit tacky, perhaps, but why squeeze around an eight-person table 364 days a year just to avoid being tacky on the 365th?

Consider the size of a chest of drawers. How many people are going to use it? Is there a closet in the same room that can take some of the clothes? What is going to be stored most of the time in the drawers? If two people are going to share it, two tiers of small drawers side by side are best. They are more convenient than assigning one person to the two top drawers and another to the two bottom drawers, especially if small things like socks and handkerchiefs are to be kept there.

Another example of where careful planning will avoid a lot of tears is in the matter of a kitchen table. Since many modern kitchens are small, the size of the table and its chairs are critical, as are their design. For example, the difference between a 50" x 54" tabletop and a 54" x 60" tabletop is only a few square inches. But in many instances this may be just enough difference to keep a plump person from even getting between the table and a wall. Some kitchen tables have legs at an angle, with their lower ends farther apart than perfectly vertical legs would be. Certainly not the design to select for close quarters. Get a kitchen table with perfectly vertical legs. They take a minimum of floor area and interfere least with people sitting down and getting up. By the same measure, captain's chairs, which are beautiful, take up a lot more space than armless, straight-back kitchen chairs.

Wall space. Much of our furniture is designed to back up against a wall. The reason for this is the need in modern, small homes to keep as much floor space free for walking, etc., as possible. Since house walls include doors, windows, radiators, and sometimes fireplaces, most homes and apartments do not have too much wall space to begin with. In addition, whatever free wall space you may see or actually measure, it is almost always less than it appears to be.

You have to take into account the depth of the furniture that is backed up against a wall. For example, a sideboard may be 24 inches deep. If you place the edge of the sideboard flush with the side of a window, some of the light and air will be blocked. In addition, the window will look blocked in. So you must keep the sideboard—or couch or chair—some distance away from the edge of the window. The same holds true for a doorway. Thus you have anywhere up to one foot less wall space than may measure out on one or both sides of doorways and windows.

Radiators are an even worse problem. You should never back furniture up against a radiator. The heat will ruin the furniture and the furniture will block the heat flow out of the radiator, chilling the room and wasting fuel. You need at least 18 inches of clearance around any radiator.

You should not place the edges of furniture flush against the sides of a fireplace opening because the heat of the fire will damage the furniture and block the flow of heat as well. The radiant heat and sparks from a fireplace could also set fire to too closely placed furniture.

To determine how close to a wall opening you can place furniture, simulate the space the furniture will occupy with a piece of newspaper. Fasten it in place with a little tape; then move the paper simulators about until they are satisfactory. You can now measure the actual space that you have to work with. Using these figures you can determine the maximum and, to some extent, the minimum sizes of the against-the-walls furniture you should buy. If you have a true 100 clear inches of wall and you want a 72-inch long couch to go there, you know by simple math that you cannot fit an end table wider than 28 inches in the remaining space.

On the other hand, if you just measure the wall space without allowing for the projection of the furniture into the room, you may believe you have 120 or more useful inches of wall space, when actually you have only 100.

ALMOST READY TO GO

At this point you know the maximum total amount you want to spend; approximately how much of that is allotted to each piece of furniture; the size of the furniture; the function it has, and its general design. Next you need to fill in details such as color, material, design, style, etc. This is covered in the following chapter.

2

Putting It All Together

For the sake of discussion, we shall assume that you are starting your interior decorating with a bare slate. Your rooms are empty, and there is nothing on the floors.

BEGIN AT THE BEGINNING

This advice may appear to be gratuitous, but it is not. Many people begin their home decorating planning on what they have seen at a friend's house, in magazines, museums, and furniture dealer's showrooms. Whether you would like to "do" your home in authentic Regency or Early American Thrift Shop, the place to begin is with people. Who will occupy the rooms? How many occupants will there be? How long will they spend in there? What will they do there?

Each room has a purpose. Will your kitchen be used exclusively for cooking? Will you have breakfast there? How many people would usually be eating there at one time? Does "breakfast" mean coffee and toast to your family, or a large, hearty meal? Will a tiny table or even a small bar, and stools do, or do you need a lot of space?

If the kitchen is small, perhaps it would be best to place a small work table in the kitchen and plan to have sturdy dining room furniture, with nonupholstered chairs.

If you are going to take all your meals in the dining room you should consider a large sideboard with generous storage space for dishes, silver, and the like.

Think these things out from the point of view of the people involved; their likes, dislikes, and habits, and not because of the sale on kitchen or dining room furniture some shop may be running.

Sloppy, neat or in between? Now, while the rooms and floors are still bare, is the time to determine your own and your family's personalities and how they will affect the home furnishings.

There are people who love to dress for dinner even if they live in a two-room apartment and dine alone. They enjoy formality, sitting upright in a beautiful chair, surrounded by order and elegance.

On the other hand, if you and your family enjoy walking about the house with your shoes off, you would be well advised to consider carefully just how much time you and your family expect to spend in the living room and just how comfortable you want to be. If informality is your mode of life, you would choose, for example, a couch covered in one of the many plastics rather than silk brocade. You'd choose a nylon rug rather than a Persian or wool.

CHILDREN AND OTHER LOVELY BEASTIES

Children and dogs and cats are happy facts of many of our lives. Dogs shed; cats often scratch; both sometimes lose control and urinate, defecate or regurgitate where they shouldn't. Children, too, are not housebroken in the beginning; when they are, they still like to climb, tear, kick and race through the house, endangering the furniture. Take it from us, who have lived with children and pets, children can cause infinitely more damage.

Childproof furniture. You can furnitureproof the child, or childproof the furniture.

We remember visiting a woman who decorated the tops of her furniture with thick paint. She squeezed various colors from selected tubes of artist's colors into a decorative pattern. Since the paint was very thick—as thick as cord—it formed a bas-relief of sorts, but took years to dry.

"Don't your young children ever touch the still soft paint?" we asked. "I'll break their arms if they do, and they know it," she answered.

This is one approach. The other is to childproof the furniture. Select durable furniture with thick, heavy legs; little children will sometimes bite thin furniture legs, just the way little dogs do. Or, purchase comparatively inexpensive, used furniture that will serve its purpose until your children grow up. Then introduce the delicate, beautiful furniture you love.

Install a minimum of furniture. The fewer pieces the less to be damaged. The more open space the less likely that the children will run into the furniture. Beware of small-bottomed pedestal stands, floor lamps, and the like. They are too easily knocked over.

Don't lay down wall-to-wall carpeting when you have a baby in the crawling stage or young children. No matter what any salesman tells you, a carpet is never as clean as a bare floor and children don't particularly need soft floors to walk or crawl on. And should an area of the carpeting be permanently stained, it is almost impossible to replace a section without the patch showing.

Rugs, on the other hand, one way or another, can always be washed. So if you must have something on the floor, opt for what can be cleaned and replaced comparatively economically.

CEILINGS, WALLS AND FLOORS ARE IMPORTANT

Most homes have flat ceilings that are or should be painted white. White blends with everything and reflects the most light. Almost anything will "go" under such ceilings. The flat, white ceiling just floats up there intent upon itself.

Half-timbered ceilings (those where a portion of the rafters shows through the plaster) and completely exposed rafter ceilings, as you would see on the underside of an unfinished attic roof or converted barn, dominate the room. You see the half-timbered and the exposed rafter ceilings as soon as you enter, so whatever is placed beneath must "belong" or it looks out of place. They call for provincial or 15th- to 18th-century antique-styled furnishing—and perhaps even something as late as American Federal. Such ceilings were common in both Europe and America during these times and can still be found in European cottages and farmhouses.

The bare underside of an attic or a barn roof always turns brown with time as the wood oxidizes. Anything that could conceivably be considered farm, provincial, or rustic can be used here, but plastic modern or even Art Deco styles would look out of place. So would "soft" furniture and upholstered antiques (or reproductions) from most periods. The overall color of the furniture should blend with the soft brown of the roof's underside.

Choosing a ceiling color. Unless you have some special situation, white and off-white are the best colors to use on a ceiling. Any other color, except the color of exposed roofing planks and rafters, will come as a shock and surprise. Green might be pleasing in a room filled with plants that reach the ceiling. In such a room a bright blue, suggesting the sky might also be pleasant. But not in a room filled with everyday furniture.

Floor colors. The color of any floor is the color of its topmost surface. We mention this to prevent confusion. A wood floor of white oak is pale yellow; covered with a maroon wall-to-wall carpet, the color of the floor becomes maroon.

In floors you have a far wider choice of colors than that for colors used on ceilings. Floor colors range from a dark, brown mahogany color to almost pure white. Before we go further we would like to clear up a common misconception concerning color and soil. Many believe that a dark floor is easier to keep clean than a light floor. The converse is true. Soil is generally light tan in color. Thus a light-colored floor shows less soil than a dark-colored floor, and a tan floor shows the least soil, which is why the color beige is so popular for rugs. (Beige also blends well with many colors.)

The color of wood floors varies. White oak looks pale yellow. Red oak is a pale red-yellow. The teaks are varying shades of dark brown.

All bare wood can be stained a darker color, but once it has been stained it is almost impossible to lighten, as the stain soaks too deeply into the wood. Bleach affects only the top surface of the wood. And bleach, be warned, softens the wood. So if you have a dark floor and want a lighter one, think about covering it with a rug. If you have a light-colored floor and wish to darken it, all the varnish and previous waxes must be ground off and the surface made smooth before the stain is applied. This is something you can do by yourself with a rented floor scraper (sanding machine). Rent the largest you can find (it works best), and make certain you go all the way to the edges or your stain job will come out uneven.

Dark or light floors. Dark is somber, formal. Light is gay, frivolous. A library, with shelves filled with books, deep, dark leather couches and chairs, old desks and small reading lamps will profit by a dark floor. On the other hand Swedish Modern blond maple furniture would look wrong sitting on a dark floor, no matter how ornate and beautiful the floor itself might be.

What about a light-colored rug beneath light furniture atop a dark floor? The answer would depend on the contrast. A very dark floor around a very light rug would be dramatic. If the basic purpose of the arrangement was display, as for example in a shop window or in a manufacturer's showroom, the combination might work. But in one's home this startling contrast would soon become annoying. This, by the way, is a very important facet of the art of interior decorating; will it work day in and day out?

On the other hand, if the floor is only somewhat darker than the rug, and the rug is not *very* light but of a color that blends with the floor, contrast between rug and surrounding floor might add to the overall attractiveness of the room. It is a matter of degree, and of course taste.

A dark rug on a light floor can be dramatic, but the rug should be interesting enough to deserve the attention it will get.

Carrying this theme a bit further, there is the color relationship of the furniture to the rug to consider. With a dark floor and light rug, what would be best for the furniture? It depends upon the degree of contrast. A small or light contrast would probably heighten the beauty of the arrangement; extreme contrast would without a doubt reduce it.

Dark furniture on a light rug would increase the visual contrast between the rug and the floor.

We can see also that the color of the floor dominates the room and must be included in your preliminary decorating and furniture decisions.

Choosing a wall color. Walls dominate a room even more than do its floor and ceiling. If you want to hide your furniture, paint the wall the same color. But if you want to "present" your furniture, choose a very pale shade of a color that will allow the furniture to stand out. Do not choose a "beautiful" color.

This is a mistake many people furnishing a home for the first time often make. The paint salesman hands them a chart with many color "chips" on it. Each color is more beautiful

Moderately dark floor and walls nicely set off the light furniture and rug and the room's predominately light paintings.

than the next. But, as artists say, each color is almost saturated —just as bright as modern chemistry will allow. On an entire wall, the color will be oppressive. There is just too much of it, and nothing will blend in; nothing will look good against such strongly colored walls. (There is one exception, which we shall discuss shortly.)

How bright should your wall colors be? Instead of the usual recipe for mixing colors—one ounce of liquid color to one gallon of white paint—we can only suggest that a fourth that amount of color is usually more than enough.

A little gray or a little umber and white is called off-white or eggshell, and it goes with everything. Many paint companies manufacture these pale shades and offer them ready-mixed. The others are made by adding a little color to white and mixing. It is easy. Blue is a poor choice as you usually have to add so much to make the color's presence felt that you have a "strong" color on your wall. The same is true of the reds, which, of course, when added to white makes pink, and of the mauves, made by adding purple to white.

Just be careful as to how much color you add. You can't remove it, and it takes gallons of white to lighten.

A word about white. White and off-white are never just that. The paint doesn't change color, but it reflects all the colors that strike it. Thus in early morning your white walls will glow pink. In the pause of midday the walls may reflect a kind of violet, and in the evening you may see strong mauves on your white walls. But meanwhile, the white reflects all the colors of the nearby objects and furniture. More than any other color—and of course, technically, white is not classified as a color—white shows more tints, more reflections and color changes as light changes than does any other single color.

Color variations. If you believe that white or off-white is much too tame, and want something stronger, here is a suggestion. Paint three walls of a room white, and the fourth wall a moderately saturated color. Then, depending on the movement of light, the other walls will change and reflect some of the color some of the time.

When you want one wall to look farther away than the rest, paint it a darker color.

Dark walls. When you plan to hang a tapestry or a light-colored rug, you can heighten the effect by painting the wall a dark color. The result is a kind of frame around the hanging.

However, this only works when the hanging occupies much of the wall. If the rug is only 6 feet wide and the wall is 12 feet wide, for example, the result is not a border, but a dark wall in the room.

Choose your dark wall carefully. It must blend with or support the color of the hanging. If you are hanging a Persian rug, with intricate and intertwined colors, stand far enough away from it (or remove your glasses) for the pattern to fuse into a single color, and use that color as your guide. It is dominant.

The earth colors go well with almost all other colors. The reds, blues, and greens take more care. Look at your colors.

The neutral-colored near monotones of the rug, walls and furniture provide an excellent setting for the dramatic painting on the wall.

You may have heard that red doesn't go with green. But there isn't one red, there are many, and one may be just right with your particular green.

A simple pretest. To check the visual results of, say, a light rug on a dark floor, find a piece of cardboard or paper as near as possible to the color of your floor. (Magazines or empty cartons are a good source.) Then lay a second piece of cardboard, matching the rug you are considering atop the first piece. To find the visual effect of the furniture you are considering, cut some strips from a third piece of cardboard that matches your contemplated furniture and place them on top of the "rug" cardboard.

You can do the same with wall colors. Try your paint on a piece of cardboard, or secure cardboard of the correct color and place strips to represent furniture against it.

Designers of stage sets often build their set in miniature first. You don't have to go this far, but a few simple walls and floors of cardboard on which you position small boxes to suggest furniture can be of tremendous help in developing an overall color scheme.

SPACE IS ALSO A DECORATING CONSIDERATION

To a great extent your choice of furniture design is limited by the space available. If the room is fairly large—say more than 20 feet by 20 feet or so—you have more or less of a free hand in the selection of style. When the room is smaller, you are constrained to fill it with pieces that do not dwarf the room or restrict passage through it.

Most modern homes and apartments do not have rooms this large. To cram a smaller room with heavy-legged Tudor style or Spanish Renaissance pieces is to reduce their effectiveness seriously.

Unfortunately there is no rule of thumb that lets you know in advance just how crowded a room will look when certain pieces are installed. You may need more than just sufficient walk and work space. The more massive a piece of furniture is, the more it must be surrounded by its own open space.

It might seem that you could make a reasonably accurate assumption by the size of the room in which the pieces are displayed, but you cannot decide on that basis alone. For example, if you see in a show room a heavy refectory table with but two or four chairs, measure the room in which it stands and then compare these measurements to your own room, to make an evaluation. And remember that mirrors, pictures on the walls, drapes all tend to reduce the room visually. The same table and chairs in an otherwise bare room will appear to have much less space if the walls carry paintings and the like. Doors and windows detract from the sense of space, even though they do not physically interfere with the use of the furniture.

The only guide we can give you is that you think of providing twice the minimum clearance necessary if you believe the furniture is "heavy," one-and-a-half times the minimum clearance if you consider the furniture to be moderately heavy, and at least the minimum clearance if you consider the furniture to be "light."

Dark furniture appears to be heavier and thicker than it

may actually be; light-colored furniture appears to be thinner and lighter. But just what constitutes dark, light, heavy, and moderate, cannot be measured. Your only guide here is your own response to the furniture.

Minimum clearances. The average male, wearing the usual indoor winter clothing, including a suit jacket, has a shoulder span of about 26 inches. Thus walkabout space must be a minimum of about 30 inches if a man is not going to feel constrained to walk sideways between pieces of furniture. If two pedestal tables are alongside one another, the 30 inches of clearance should be between their tops, not their legs.

Seat depth on a nonupholstered chair is usually about 15 inches, but because the back of many chairs tilt, the average "hard" chair occupies 22 inches or so front to back. The average adult male needs about 8 inches of leg room. Thus you need a minimum of 30 inches between the edge of a tabletop and an adjacent wall. Less space and you will have to bend your knees and get out from your seat by moving sideways.

Limited space. Where space is limited you are automatically forced to select furniture with thin legs, airy graceful shapes, and light colors. Each piece of furniture, however, must be full size. There is little sense in buying undersized chairs and tables. At the other extreme, if the room is very large and you want a minimum number of pieces, it is usually better to select heavy, dark furniture. If you prefer light furniture, you can use more pieces. But since few furniture shops will accept returns, you are well advised to start with a minimum of furniture in a large room and add pieces as you find desirable.

MAKE THE BASIC DECISIONS FIRST

Decide now whether the room or rooms are to be formal; semiformal, or casual. Within these broad categories, do you want the furniture to be heavy and dark or thin and light?

What style? Within the restrictions you have so far set up; what style or period would you like best? Or, what period best suits your basic needs?

Most of us can answer these questions very easily. There are hundreds of illustrated books on furniture to refer to and also many museums.

Few of us, however, can finance the answer to these questions as easily. Well, since authentic pieces and high-quality reproductions are equally out of reach, what is available at a price we can manage? Put crudely, this is the moment of compromise.

Bear in mind that to look good, furniture does not have to duplicate any period or style exactly. It need only have the flavor of that period, whether long-ago or yesterday. To be beautiful, a room need not reflect or duplicate a period in furniture history.

One compromise is to start with one super-excellent piece, for example, a beautiful Queen Anne reproduction of museum quality, and say to hell with the rest. It can be orange crates if there is nothing left in the thrift shops. Then each year add another authentic, museum-quality reproduction until the entire house is veritably a museum itself. This works, if you don't mind spending most of your life on orange crates while you view one or two beautiful pieces of furniture and save for more.

The alternative compromise consists of looking at ads, visiting showrooms, and the homes of friends, etc. This requires time and effort. After a while you will develop a mental picture of what is available in your price range, and you will be able to visualize it somewhat in your home.

But, *most important*, the furniture in a room should look part of a whole.

A heavy-legged table calls for heavy-legged chairs and sideboard. A formal room calls for a minimum of curves and straight-backed chairs. Don't let the inability to let go of something good that you own restrict you. "We want to do our bedroom in Early American, but we have this wonderful Victorian brass bed Aunt Tillie left us." If you don't want to tell guests to whom you show your home that Ben Franklin in-

How formal do you want your room to be? The heavy, patterned furniture, dark walls and figured drapes complement the sedate marble fireplace. The total effect is very formal.

A comfortable room, but not one for everyday family rough-and-tumble.

A true family room, with its sturdy furniture and easy, lived-in look.

vented the brass bed and that is why it is in your Early American bedroom, sell it. Use the money to buy the furniture you want.

Sets. There are some 500 furniture manufacturers in this country alone, and most of them offer sets or groupings with elegant, exciting titles. There are advantages and disadvantages to purchasing these sets. Often you do not want or need nor can you fit all of the pieces in a set into your home, but you must take all or nothing. You may want additional pieces, but the manufacturer does not make additional pieces for the set, and the pieces of the set are so characteristic that you cannot bring in a different piece. Very often this identification of one piece with another is so strong that it is visually oppressive. A couch covered in red plaid, chairs the same, even a coffee table with a piece of the same material glued to its top and covered by glass, can easily be disastrous.

On the plus side, it is easier to let the manufacturer match the pieces for you. Generally there is some saving in purchasing several pieces at one time from one source.

ALL-AMERICAN CLUTTER

The Victorians were probably the first to ignore style and make their homes informal museums. This was a time of public interest in science, a time when a journey to a foreign land was more than a short plane ride, and people were proud to display the mementos they brought back. Thus the better homes of this period were rather cluttered, and a typical parlor might display stuffed birds in glass cases, mineral collections, African spears, carved whalebone, a telescope on a tripod and more.

Often the furniture was collected rather than assembled to suit someone's taste or decorating scheme. Some pieces were upholstered in leather; some in cloth; straight-backed, hard-seat chairs stood alongside soft couches.

It is a personal matter whether or not you like this "collection" approach to interior decorating. Some find it charming and enjoy living in such mismatched surroundings; others abhor the ill-assorted mixture.

There are a number of advantages to following no style or all styles when furnishing your home. Whatever piece you add, so long as it is in itself attractive, will fit your nondecorating

Flowered upholstery is repeated on the large background screens and complemented by the sculptured rug, the flowers in the fireplace and even the legs of the coffee table. They combine to give a cheerful, airy look; the pattern is not so large that it overwhelms.

scheme. Since you need never purchase more than one piece at a time, and used furniture fits in well, you don't run the risk involved in buying a set or a collection that you may find you do not like after a while. You can add and remove pieces whenever you like.

ANCILLARY FURNISHINGS

Curtains. Curtains are hung to shield one's home from the vision of others, but an equally important function is to make a room more attractive.

Curtains do this in two ways: They soften incoming light; diffuse and spread it so that shadows are not quite as dark and the light is nowhere as bright as direct daylight. They also provide a change of texture and color on the wall, and this fact is most important in decorating a room.

The color of the curtain must be considered in relation to the color of the walls and the colors or major color of the furniture. In a formal room the curtain should be of a single color and subdued, but not necessarily dark. In an informal room a curtain's color can be somewhat brighter, but it should not be so bright and gay that it dominates the room. There has to be a balance. It is a mistake to purchase and hang curtains that are so beautiful they are works of art in themselves. You want to present a room as a whole and not as a background for a curtain.

Bear in mind that the curtain will be backed by light, therefore it will naturally be brighter hanging in the window than when spread over a shop's counter. The light coming through the curtain will be transformed. A red curtain will pass red light, a green curtain will pass green. Ask yourself, "Do I *want* a red or green light coming in my window?"

Drapes. Originally, drapes, which are heavy cloths, were hung over walls and windows to keep out the cold. Thus drapes are traditionally of fairly thick cloth that provides some insulation. They were usually of a somber color to reduce the necessity of frequent washing.

Warmth and the hiding of soil are no longer of prime importance. Drapes can be of any color we wish and of any weight or weave that hangs well.

Like curtains, drapes alter the texture and color of the wall by replacing some or all of it. But drapes also frame windows and can be used to change the appearance of a wall as you like.

The color of drapes can be anything from an exact match of the wall color to a strong contrast. In some cases the color and texture of a drape is carried over the window in the form of a valance. Think of the word "frame" here as being used in the exact sense of a picture frame.

To alter the appearance of the entire wall you can draw the drapes across it and the window, so that they form columns at either end of the wall during part of the day, and cover the entire wall at other times. With such an arrangement you can have fairly dark drapes because the two columns do not clash visually with the furniture.

WALL HANGINGS

All sorts of things have been hung on walls in times past for ornamentation and warmth.

Tapestries were used to insulate the cold stone walls of castles. Today, one sees walls hung with colorful rugs; Persian, American Indian, Mexican, Israeli and others. To select and position wall hangings, follow the principles already outlined. The overall or basic color should reinforce the basic color scheme of the walls and furniture. The style should supplement the general style of the furniture, but only if the hanging is very large and dominates a wall. If the hanging is small, in relation to the wall space, it may be treated like a painting.

Almost all paintings will work on almost all walls. The exceptions are very large oils with only a few, very dominant colors. These you will find mainly in the field of nonrepresentational art. In any event, if you want to hang a large bright green or bright red painting, you had best give the painting a test run on the wall.

Painting of almost any color and type under 2 by 3 feet in size will go anywhere. You can balance a pair on either side of a fireplace, hang one above another alongside a door, place a series in ascending heights on a wall. It is almost impossible to position paintings poorly on any wall. In any case, it is easy enough to hang them temporarily and see what they do or do not do for the room.

Growing plants are wonderful room ornaments, and it is impossible to go wrong with them. Everything green looks beautiful and will enhance the room it graces.

3

Wood and Wood Joinery

Despite the increasing popularity of metals and plastics in the making of furniture, at least among manufacturers, wood is still the most frequently used material and is likely to remain so for a long time. Since at least a dozen different kinds of wood are commonly used for making furniture, and there are considerable differences between woods in strength, durability and beauty, it is important to know a little about them and to be able to recognize them when we purchase furniture.

And since no furniture is stronger than its joints, it is also necessary to know a little about furniture construction—wood joinery, to use an old term—when we evaluate furniture.

(Materials other than wood are discussed in the chapters dealing with furniture made from them.)

HARDWOODS AND SOFTWOODS

The hardwoods are broad-leafed trees, such as maple and oak. Long pores or tubes run the length of the tree's trunk and limbs. These pores are easily seen when the wood is dried and cut across its grain. The pores on oak, for example, are particularly large.

Softwood trees have narrow leaves, or needles. Conifers, which are evergreen, and which most of us call simply pine are softwood trees. They have no pores in their trunks.

Unfortunately, the wood of these trees is not always consonant with their classification. Some "hardwoods," such as the poplar and sycamore, are softer than some of the soft-woods.

Test. You can recognize wood that is truly hard in a number of ways. One method, obviously, is to recognize the wood by its color, grain structure, and grain pattern. Another is to test the wood for hardness by forcing a knife point into it (on the underside of the furniture, of course). You will have great difficulty forcing a knife point into oak or maple; you will have no trouble at all with pine. You can even indent pine with the end of your fingernail.

Weight is another practical method of identifying wood.

WEIGHT OF VARIOUS KINDS OF WOOD

TYPE	POUNDS PER CUBIC FOOT
White pine	22-31
Walnut	40-43
Ash	43-53
Oak	37-56
Beech	43-56
Apple	41-52
Box	59-72
African teak	61
Ebony	67-83
Lignum Vitae	73-83

As you can see, white pine weighs roughly half as much as walnut, oak, apple, and beech. The real hardwoods, box, teak, ebony and lignum vitae, are very dense, or heavy. (Some varieties sink in water.)

Color is no indication, unless you know the wood and its markings or "figuring"—the patterns the grain makes. Most softwoods are light in color, but some "colored" woods are also soft. For example, cedar, cypress and luan (sometimes passed off as Philippine mahogany) are reddish and are soft. Maple is a pale yellow and very hard.

In furniture 80 or more years old, you can identify the wood by the width of the boards used. If they are more than 6 or 8 inches wide, chances are the wood is not a hardwood, because many of the hardwoods were taken from small-bore trees. Even when the wood was comparatively plentiful, not many broad hardwood boards were used. Instead, narrow strips were glued side to side to make the wide board.

(If you are interested in knowing more about wood identification, write to A. Constantine, 2050 Eastchester Road, Bronx, N.Y. 10464. Among other things of interest to woodworkers, they sell samples of the various furniture woods.)

The harder, the better. The hardwoods are much more desirable for furniture than the softwoods for many reasons. They are stronger, much more resistant to abrasions and identation; they are more easily polished, and some, like teak and ebony, resist rot. Hardwood can be made smoother than softwood can, and whatever varnish is applied will stand up to time and wear much better on hardwood than on soft. Varnish—and for the moment we include all the finishes in this definition—is not strong. It must be supported. When applied to softwood, the least pressure indents the wood and cracks the varnish.

Some of the hardwoods, like teak, contain natural oil so that they look as though they are lightly varnished even when they are not.

And last, but certainly far from least, all the hardwoods are more beautiful than the softwoods.

Comparative costs. Hardwoods always cost more than softwoods. A tree that weighs 80 pounds per square foot takes four times longer to grow to size than a tree that weighs 20 pounds per square foot. Another reason is that most of the hardwoods grow overseas in tropical countries. It is estimated there are 75% as many trees in America now as when Columbus arrived, but most of the hardwoods are gone. American walnut, for example, is so scarce and valuable that full-grown walnut trees have been "rustled" from the front lawns of home owners when they were away.

Comparative value. Since manufacturer's profit, shipping costs, advertising and retailer's mark-up represent by far the greatest portion of the retail price of a piece of furniture, we believe it is foolish to save the small difference that may exist between hardwood furniture and softwood furniture.

At this writing there is a considerable quantity of imitation Spanish dining room furniture being offered, made of knotty pine. The pine has been stained a dark brown; the pieces are thick and very substantial looking. But if a guest taps the handle of his fork against the table, or you drop a plate and the edge hits the tabletop, a dent will mark the spot.

There is something to be said for pine, however. It was the wood many of our ancestors used for making furniture, so if you want an authentic reproduction, it should be of pine. Don't expect it to wear well; it won't.

If we were given the choice of a good used piece of furniture made from hardwood and a new piece made from pine, we'd choose the used every time.

SOLID OR BUILT UP

The days of refectory tables and dining room tables made from a single slab of burly walnut or oak are long gone. Unless you hire a forester to find a mammoth tree and cut, haul, and dry it, you will have to be satisfied with solid tabletops built up of several pieces of wood, unless the table is very small and narrow. All, or almost all, solid furniture parts more than 6 or 8 inches wide are made of several pieces of wood glued and clamped together, then planed and treated as a single slab. And this is good, not bad.

Since a number of pieces of wood are joined side by side, the tendency of one piece of wood to warp in one direction is offset by another bending in the opposite direction. Today's glues are so strong and waterproof that a slab made of joined pieces of wood is stronger than a single slab.

In better furniture, care is taken to match the grain of the adjoining pieces. In some cases, woods of differing color are joined side by side. Butcher block furniture is a notable example of this art.

A well-made composite slab of wood shows no cracks or open spaces between the joined pieces. In fact you should have to look closely to see that more than one strip of wood has been used. If one strip of wood is loose, if there are spaces between the strips of wood, the work is defective. To repair it properly, the slab should be taken apart, reglued, resanded, and refinished, though this is not something that can be done with a few hand tools.

VENEER

Veneering is the technical name for applying a thin sheet of wood over another piece or pieces of wood. Today veneers are also made of plastic. The tabletops and other large surfaces of most modern furniture are veneered.

Advantages. Veneers, which are made from attractive hardwood, improve the appearance of furniture. The softwoods under the veneer do not take polish and finish nearly as well and are easily scuffed and dented. Veneer can be cut and positioned so that its normal pattern is enhanced. Various decorative designs can be introduced. And since the veneer is hardwood it will wear better than the softer wood underneath.

Few furniture purchasers trouble to differentiate between solid and veneer furniture. When they do, they most often select the veneer because it is usually more attractive and looks almost exactly like a piece made entirely of the wood used in the veneer. In other words a table in cherry veneer looks almost like a table made of solid cherry. The difference would be in the edges in that you would see the end grain on the solid. On the veneer, you would see a strip of veneer covering the ends of the boards.

Disadvantages. Veneered surfaces are unsuited to hard, constant use and can be damaged by constant wetting. A veneered dining room table that is to be on display most of the year and used only on holidays will last for generations, but the same table would not last long in a busy kitchen. In time, unnoticed spills would loosen the veneer. Once that happens, it is difficult to restore the piece to its original beauty. Hot cooking pots mistakenly placed on a veneer surface do no more damage than on a solid wood surface, but you can sand down the burns and dents in solid wood and refinish it, but you cannot do this with veneer. It is too thin.

Plastic veneer. Plastic veneer has been used in furniture making for at least 30 years. Originally, it was mainly used on kitchen cabinet counter tops, then on kitchen tables. Today we find this material topping coffee tables, desks, and even dining room tables.

The high-pressure plastics, Formica, Micarta and others, are very hard and shiny, and resist abrasion and heat. They come in a large variety of bright colors and patterns. A few years ago, manufacturers introduced these and other somewhat softer plastics in wood colors, with simulated grain and finely textured surfaces. They can pass as natural wood if you do not look too closely.

These plastic veneers are all tough, wear better and are more heat-resistant than any natural wood. We can only evaluate plastic veneer by the quality of the workmanship expended to apply it. Look for tables with plastic, not metal edges. Examine these edges carefully. The edge strips must be tight. The joint between edge and top must be straight and even all the way around. There can be no bubbles or loose areas in the plastic any more than in wood veneer. If there are bubbles or if the veneer is in any way loose, do not buy the piece. There is no easy way of making a repair.

While the plastic veneers will last many years, eventually their top surface becomes scuffed and the color and pattern worn. When this happens there is no practical way of effecting a repair. By comparison, a solid oak-top table can be sanded down and revarnished. The inherent character of plastic veneer deters many buyers. No matter how bright the color, it still looks and feels like plastic.

PLYWOOD

Plywood is wood that is constructed of three or more layers (or "plies") of thin wood glued together. The inexpensive grades come apart in water. The top grades are so unaffected by water that they are used for boat hulls. Plywood is made in a tremendous range of woods, thicknesses, and qualities. Since the surface of plywood is a thin layer of veneer, plywood comes in a wide range of surface woods. When the edge of a piece of plywood is left unfinished, you can see the plies. The more of these a board has, the better.

Most modern furniture contains some plywood; usually the side panels on bureaus; drawer bottoms, backs and so on. There is nothing wrong with plywood, but when it is very thin and obviously ready to come apart, stay clear of it.

CRAFTSMAN VERSUS MACHINE

Wood is still joined to wood in the same limited number of ways first introduced by the Egyptians. The only difference is that today machines make most of the joints and our glues are considerably better than the ancient glues.

Any argument a salesperson may put forth as to the superiority of handmade joints over machine-made joints is false. If two pieces of furniture are identical—same wood, same thickness, same hardware, same finish and size, the machine-made furniture is slightly better than the handmade furniture. Since a machine can cut joints more accurately, machine-made joints are stronger. (However, handmade furniture may be superior in other ways. It is most often made of solids, thick boards which include some touch of the craftsman's hand.)

In machine-made furniture, machines are used only in the cutting of the joints; the fitting, gluing, etc. is still done by hand. (This is a simplification, but essentially true.)

TYPES OF WOOD JOINTS

Furniture is usually made with one or more of the following joints:

Mortise and tenon. This is a basic joint type. It is employed in many variations. A hole or notch, called the mortise, is cut into one board. A projection at the end of the second board, called the tenon, fits into the mortise. Usually there is a shoulder on the tenon so that the edges of the mortise are hidden. The tenon may be square, rectangular, or round. The mortise must of course have the same shape. Sometimes the tenon is merely the tapered end of a dowel (a round stick).

The strength of these joints depends on how far the tenon extends into the mortise, how closely the parts are fitted and the quality of the glue. Rectangular and square tenons make for stronger joints than do round tenons because they cannot be turned. Turning loosens the glue.

Pegged joints. Today, glue and sometimes screws are used to hold tenons in place in the mortise. But before there was a

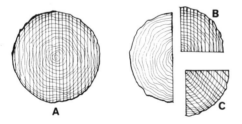

Three ways of cutting boards (straight lines) from a tree trunk give three different grain patterns (wavy lines). **A** *is a standard cut,* **B** *is quartered, and* **C** *is rift cut.*

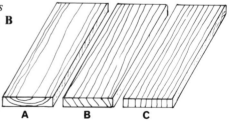

strong glue, a hole would be drilled through the side of the tenon and the surrounding wood. Then a peg would be forced through the hole to lock the tenon in place. Today pegged joints are used to add the handcrafted touch. They add very little strength beyond that of the glue used.

Doweled joints. Two round holes are drilled into the edge of one board. Two similar holes are drilled into the end of the second board. Short dowels covered with glue are pushed into the holes and the boards brought together. One board does not enter the other; only the dowels join them.

Tongue and groove. A groove is cut into the edge of a board. The groove extends the full length of the board. Next, the edge of a second board is cut so that a tongue or projection extends the full length of the board. When glue is applied to the tongue and groove and the tongue is pressed into the groove, the two boards become one. This is a type of joint almost always used with flooring and roofing or siding boards.

Spline. Grooves are cut into the sides of two boards for the full length of the boards. Then a third piece of wood is cut so

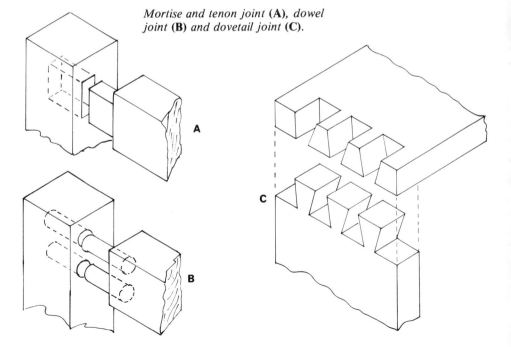

Mortise and tenon joint (A), dowel joint (B) and dovetail joint (C).

that it is as long as the two boards and just wide enough and thick enough to fit into the two grooves. This piece of wood is called a spline, and when it is covered with glue and forced into the grooves in the two boards, they are permanently joined. The spline joint wastes less wood than the tongue and groove joint; with the latter you must cut away some of the original width of the board to make the tongue.

Metal splines are also used and splines are often used to join the ends of two boards that have been mitered (cut at an angle). The resultant joint is not nearly as strong as a mortise and tenon joint.

Dovetail. This joint is used to join the ends of two boards at right angles to each other. If you put your hands together with the fingers meshing, you will more or less have a dovetail joint. This is the strongest known way of joining board ends at an angle. The joint is most often used in making drawers. By examining such a joint you can easily tell whether the piece was machine-made or handmade. A machine-made dovetail joint is perfect; every little angle is exactly like its neighbors. Handmade dovetail joints show the minor variations normal to hand work.

There are a variety of types of dovetail joints. One type is called "secret." The joint is only visible from one side. Therefore if you are examining drawers to evaluate their construction, look at both sides of each corner carefully. A really well-made secret dovetail is hard to see.

THE BIG TROUBLE WITH JOINTS

Joints are very important in the construction of furniture, but the big trouble for the buyer is that you cannot see the joints in completed furniture.

There are exceptions, of course. You can see how drawers are made if you can remove the drawers from a chest or poke your head inside to see how the piece is put together. But you usually cannot look at the outside of a joint and tell whether it is a mortise and tenon or a doweled joint. In most cases, the only time you can really tell is when the joint is coming apart, in which case it is too late.

JUDGING JOINTS

You can secure a fair estimate of the quality of the overall joinery in a piece of furniture by indirect methods. The suggestions following are not always applicable, and not always absolute indicators, but they are worth keeping in mind and applying when you can.

Heft. The comparative weight of a piece of furniture indicates to a great extent the quality of the wood used. The heavier and denser the wood, the stronger the piece generally is. When top-grade material is used, it is more than likely that the joinery is also top grade.

Overall appearance. Better-made furniture looks better-made. This is hard to explain, but if you apply this to women's clothing you will get an idea of what we mean. Better-made clothing looks better and is *finished* better: The buttons are sewn on more carefully; there are fewer loose threads; the seams are wider and so on.

This overall impression of quality can be found in fine furniture, too. Better furniture is finished more carefully; the varnish has been more evenly applied; the drawers move more smoothly and solidly, the back of the piece does not look "raw," the hardware is better; everything looks finished and solid. When you have looked at enough furniture you will be able to evaluate a piece just by a quick glance, just as a good baker can tell the quality of a shop's baked goods by smell alone.

Test the joints. Push diagonally against the corner of the chair or table. There should be no give. Try turning a chair rung or a back rung. It should be solidly in place. Try pushing and pulling apart chair legs and table legs. They should be rock-tight.

Examine the undersides. Sloppy glue application indicates sloppy workmanship; the use of nails instead of screws indicate weak joints; loose and warped pieces indicate careless manufacturing.

Examine the joints. Look closely at each joint. True, you cannot tell what has been done on the inside, but there should be no spaces between furniture parts at any joint. An open space indicates a poor fit; cracks in joined pieces near the joints possibly indicate the joint has been forced. On good furniture you may see one or two poor joints. On poor furniture you will see many of them. Once you learn how and where to look, they become obvious.

A fine old piece of cabinet work, with handcarved dovetail joints and legs. Note how the grain flows through the entire piece.

4

Kitchen Furniture

When we speak of kitchen furniture in this book we include furniture that is used in the room in which cooking is done, and also furniture used in breakfast nooks, breakfast rooms, dining alcoves, and breakfast counters. Defined by usage, breakfast furniture includes all furniture that may be used for preparing food and eating simple, nonformal meals.

KITCHENS ARE DUAL-PURPOSE PLACES

In a large kitchen all furniture doesn't have to "double in brass." Where there is room for a worktable as well as a breakfast table, the breakfast table is seldom if ever used to support a chopping board or mixing bowl. In a small kitchen one table must serve both purposes, but many people furnishing new homes fail to realize until the table is purchased and installed in the kitchen that the dual-purpose table needs more space around it than either a dining table or worktable. You need space for the chairs that are going to go around the table, and then you need space into which you can move the chairs so that you can get to the table and work on it.

In a small kitchen you will have to compromise if there isn't sufficient space for table, chairs, and work area. If you spend much time in your kitchen, select simpler, smaller designs and fewer chairs. The kitchen will be occupied but a fraction of the day for meals, whereas you will be busy working most of the day. There is nothing more time wasting and fatiguing than walking around obstacles or moving them all day long.

HOW MANY WILL YOU ACCOMMODATE?

The decision as to whether you want one or two tables in your kitchen depends not only on the size of the room but on how many people you want to feed at one time. If this number is fixed and you are going to be crowded while serving and even when working, it is best to forgo the worktable and purchase a sturdier kitchen table. (Incidentally, counter tops beneath wall cabinets are almost useless as working space.)

Infrequent guests. If you sometimes have additional mouths to feed in the kitchen and wish to prepare for them, get either a slightly larger kitchen table or one with leaves or drops, and folding chairs you can store in the attic or basement. The more walk space you have in your kitchen the easier it will be to work there and, perhaps surprisingly, the easier it will be to clean the room.

How many can you seat comfortably? Measure the part of the kitchen floor free of fixed appliances and make a reasonably accurate scale drawing of it. This is most easily done on graph paper. Adults need about 5 square feet of floor space for themselves and the chair they sit on. They need another 2.5 square feet of table on which to eat: a minimum width of 20 inches and about 30 inches of clearance between the edge of the table and the nearest wall so as to be able to sit down and get up comfortably.

It would seem that all you need do is multiply the width of the floor by its length in feet to get the square footage of the kitchen floor, and then divide it by 7.5, the chair and table area needed, to find the maximum number of people the kitchen can accommodate at a meal. But this does not leave space for walking, entrances, etc.

For a realistic figure you need to allow for refrigerator doors that may be swung open during a meal, a safety area of at least 2 feet from the back of the nearest seated person to the front of the stove. You'll need the same work space in front of the kitchen sink, and another foot and a half of clearance between the backs of those seated and the wall cabinets. In addition, you may want to allow space for someone at the far side of the table to walk around the others seated there.

So, with this in mind, enclose an area on your floor plan indicating the breakfasters and *then* divide the enclosed area by 7.5. This gives you a fairly accurate figure.

KITCHEN TABLE SHAPES AND SIZES

The importance of shape. The most efficient shape for a small table is a square with its corners rounded off. The rounded corners make it easier for us to get around the table. The square shape provides four diners with equal dining space. Unfortunately, few if any small square tables are now made with rounded corners; so we have to settle for square corners. The square table is space-efficient up to about 30 by 30 inches, the usual size of a bridge table. When the square gets larger, there is extra space in the center, which is wasteful of floor space.

When you select a rectangular table, it must be a minimum of 22 inches wide and at least 40 inches long if it is to be useful to four people sitting face to face.

When you need to seat people at the end of a rectangular table, the table should be at least 30 inches wide, and its length should be increased to a minimum of 60 inches.

Round tables are cute but inefficient. Following is an estimate of the number of people that can be seated at round tables of various diameters.

NUMBER OF PEOPLE	TABLE DIAMETER
4 to 5	36 (inches)
5 to 6	42
6 to 7	50
7 to 8	55
8 to 9	63
9 to 10	70

Round tables waste space in two ways. There are very few circular kitchens, so unless you fill the corner openings left by placing a round table in the center of the room, the corners of the room are wasted. (Of course, you may like the open space, in which case, it is not a waste.) Individuals need about 15 or so inches of table depth at each place for eating. With a 70-inch-diameter round table, for example, there is a circular 40 inches in diameter in the center of the table that is not absolutely necessary. If you are pressed for space, this is a waste. (If you are not, this is an excellent location for any of the unclassified artwork you have received as a wedding or anniversary present.)

When you get down to very small circular tables, you will find the pedestal foot that supports the top a pain. It will get in the way of your feet.

If you are a romantic and/or have the space, round tables are fine. If not, temper your enthusiasm with caution.

Incidentally, if you are uncertain of whether or not you can comfortably sit a number of people around a table you are considering, the shop should be willing to let you borrow some test chairs for a few moments. Place these around the table and actually seat yourself and see if you are comfortable.

TABLETOPS

Tabletops are made of wood, plastic, metal, glass, and marble. Obviously costs vary with material, material thickness and overall size and shape, with time, condition, and the individual shop. Which is best for you is a matter of taste and proposed use. Which type of top offers you the most for your money cannot be spelled out here. All we can do is provide you with the relative advantages and disadvantages of each.

Wood. A solid, hardwood tabletop, 1 inch or more thick, is best for a combination worktable and dining table. The thickness of the wood provides the mass that keeps the table from bouncing when you work on it. The hardwood can take punishment without showing too much wear. When the varnish does wear through, you can sand down the top and revarnish it fairly easily. You can opt to leave the tabletop bare. The hardwood will not stain readily; if it does, the color will not seep deeply into the wood, as it will with a softwood.

Rock maple and birch are used most often and are most desirable. Oak is not soft, but it is porous. A solid tabletop can be made of a number of strips of wood glued side by side. This is the way the so-called butcher block tabletops are made. (The true butcher block table is made of strips of wood glued side by side and fused in a *vertical position*.) Butcher-block-type tabletops are very strong and long lasting. They are expensive, but one way you may beat their high cost is to purchase the top separately from a restaurant supply house and add your own legs.

Today a number of furniture companies are touting pine-topped kitchen tables, including very overpriced antiques or semiantiques. Pine is soft, and filled with knots. The manufacturer says these are decorative, but they are hard. So not only do the tables wear rapidly, but with time the knots will stand higher than the rest of the surface. The result is a lumpy, bumpy tabletop not conducive to keeping cups and glasses upright.

Even if the wood is free of knots, pine and similar softwoods dent under the slightest pressure. Dents and gouges are too deep to sand down easily. Pine, being soft, does not support varnish very well, and is easily stained by coffee and tea. In our opinion a pine-topped kitchen table is a poor choice no matter how thick the pine may be. And whereas bare and worn hardwood tables have some charm, ancient softwood tables that are worn and bare look ugly.

Few kitchen tables are made of wood veneer, but sometimes people will purchase a veneered casual table or small dining room table for the kitchen. This is poor economy (unless the table is very, very inexpensive). Whether made expressly for kitchen use or originally intended for the dining room, veneer is usually glued to a soft, inexpensive wood core. Thus the veneer is not solidly supported, and will indent and break loose when you work on it. And the best of veneers have a tendency to curl up and loosen in contact with spilled coffee or other hot liquid.

Plywood differs from veneer only in that the core of the panel is composed of plies—flat sheets of wood—whereas the core of a veneered board is made of chipboard (wood chips glued together) or softwood pieces glued side by side. If all the plies in the plywood tabletop are hardwood, the plywood top is strong and nearly as good as a solid tabletop of equal thickness. If you are uncertain as to the nature of the inner plies, and the edge of the top is exposed, try testing its hardness with a small pointed instrument. If all the plies are of hardwood it should be as difficult to make an impression on the edge of the table as on its top.

Generally, plywood kitchen tabletops are not as thick a solid tops. This is not too important if you do not plan to work on the table. But we strongly advise against investing in a plywood top that is less than 5/8 inch thick. (The edge trim doesn't count. We are speaking of the actual thickness of the top itself.) It should be as close to 1 inch thick as possible, preferably even thicker. Solid tabletops of less than about 5/8 inch in thickness are not desirable investments either.

Given tabletops of equal thickness, size, and appearance, one of solid hardwood and the other of hardwood plies, we would always opt for the solid and even spend a little more for it.

Some kitchen tables and tops of wood are painted in bright colors and decorated with flowers or wood nymphs at play. If you do not plan to work on them, they will last fairly well. But remember, each time you clean these tables, you wear off some of the paint. Nicks and dents are highly visible because the wood beneath the paint is of a different color than the paint. To make these painted tables beautiful once more you have to sand the surfaces smooth and repaint. To duplicate the original finish takes lots of effort and care.

The quality of painted furniture depends not only on the quality of the paint job, something only an expert can evaluate by inspection, but on the hardness of the wood. If a table is of softwood, its paint job will deteriorate several times faster than if the same paint was on hardwood. Use a sharp instrument to test the underside of the table top.

Plastic. Today, many kitchen tabletops are made of a plastic veneer over chipboard, plywood or a glued-together, solid softwood base. Most often the veneer is Formica or Micarta, trade names for very hard, composite plastics formed under very high pressure. The surface may be smooth and shiny or may have some soft texture.

The plastic will retain its shine and underlying color and pattern for many years. But eventually, the shine will wear off, the pattern will wear and the underlying brown or gray base color will show through. A reasonable life expectancy for this kind of top is 10 to 20 years. This is far longer than any finish can last on wood under equally severe service. However, whereas you can live with bare hardwood or refinish it, once the finish on plastic is worn through or damaged by heat, that is it. It must be replaced, and this is next to impossible. Generally you have to replace the entire top or table.

The better plastic-veneered table and counter tops are edged with plastic. The less expensive and less desirable tables and counters are edged with metal. The trouble with the metal is that dirt accumulates between the plastic and the metal. The trouble with plastic edging is that a heavy blow at a corner can knock a piece off. (If you save it, you can glue it back on again with epoxy cement.)

In any case, carefully examine all plastic veneer surfaces to make certain there are no bubbles because they cannot be removed. See that all the plastic is firmly bonded in place, especially the edging. Inspect the joints between the edging and the top surface. This joint should be tight, smooth, and show an even width of material for the length of the joint. The upper vertical edge of the edging should be beveled or rounded.

Metal. Years ago, inexpensive kitchen tables of porcelainized steel were quite common. The porcelain surface was easily cleaned, difficult to scratch and crackproof so long as you didn't drop a bottle of milk or a large set of false teeth on it. Today, you may still find these tables in junk shops or even in near-antique shops. Despite their time-derived patina, they are still unattractive. As a temporary stop-gap they are fine, but as a permanent addition to a kitchen, they do not add any beauty at all.

Glass. Properly supported and sufficiently thick, glass makes an excellent dining surface. As a work surface, however, it is a poor choice. No matter how careful you may be, there is always a chance that you may break the glass, unless it is bulletproof and very thick.

Another drawback to glass in the kitchen and anywhere else is its cost. When you go to ¾-inch and thicker glass, the price goes sky high. When you select bulletproof and shatterproof glass, you are selecting glass that only gangsters and FBI agents can afford.

Marble. Now here is a luxury surface that is nearly reasonably priced. While it will lose its shine with time, you can repolish it with either a motor-driven polisher or lots of elbow grease. Its weight makes it a good work surface when completely supported, but it can be cracked and it sometimes has almost invisible flaws that lead to cracks.

By complete support we mean ¾-inch or thicker wood beneath the entire piece of marble (if you are going to work on it) and not a central pedestal with short, narrow arms reaching a fraction of the distance across the bottom of the slab.

The usual thickness is about 1 inch. Thicker is better, and thinner is only acceptable if it is fully supported, even if you do not plan to work on it.

TABLE LEGS AND GENERAL CONSTRUCTION

Table legs are made of wood or metal. They may be perfectly vertical or somewhat splayed. All of this is only important to the appearance of the table. No one leg material or manner of construction is stronger than another per se. Thin wood legs properly braced can be stronger than thick legs improperly braced or fastened.

Wood leg joinery. Legs are fastened to tabletops in any number of ways. Most common is by means of an apron, the four pieces of wood positioned on edge against the bottom of the tabletop.

Legs that are joined to an apron usually have no stretchers. A stretcher is any piece of wood or metal that stretches from one leg to another near the bottom. A stretcher is therefore a brace. When the table's legs are not braced, the joint between the legs and the apron must be very strong because the lower end of the leg can exert tremendous pressure on the joint. If, for example, you placed a table (or chair) without stretchers on its side and pushed down on the end of a leg, you would probably break that leg free.

Thus if the legs are fastened to an apron and there are no stretchers the apron should be at least 3 inches wide and at least ¾ inch thick. More is of course better.

The legs may be fastened to the apron in any of several ways. One method consists of joining the legs by mortise and tenon joints, the mortise being cut into the side of the leg. Generally, you can recognize this type of joinery by the position of the apron against the leg end. The leg projects outward from the apron by ½ inch or so. A variation often used is a dowel joint at this juncture. When a dowel joint is used here, the surface of the leg and the apron are generally flush with one another. The dowel joint is nowhere nearly as strong as the mortise and tenon joint. Unfortunately there is no certain way of determining which may be used. However, if you can see light between the apron end and the side of the leg, the joint is a dowel joint—and a poorly made one at that.

Legs are also joined to aprons by means of hanger bolts. These are bolts with a wood screw thread at one end and a machine bolt thread at the other. The ends of the apron are joined and held together by a V-block. The hanger bolt goes through a hole in the leg and is then screwed into the V-block. Then a nut is run up on the end of the hanger bolt. When the nut is tightened the leg is firmly locked in place.

This is a very strong way to fashion a corner and attach a leg. Be sure, however, that the corner block is held in place with screws as well as glue. Without the screws, the joint is weak and one good bang on the end of the leg can break it loose.

Another, but less desirable method of making the corner of the apron and fastening the leg uses a bent strip of metal that fits into grooves in the apron. When a bolt that holds the leg is tightened, the leg and the two meeting pieces of apron are pulled together. If the metal is heavy and generous in size, the joint should last a long time. But too often this type of joint is made with thin metal that gives way all too easily.

The apron itself should be fastened to the underside of the tabletop with wood screws and glue. V-blocks glued in place are not very good. The best arrangement consists of long holes drilled through the edges of the apron. Screws driven through these holes and into the underside of the tabletop can be depended upon to hold almost forever. If necessary, the screws can easily be tightened.

Some of the tables with splayed legs, made by individual craftsmen, have legs with top ends that fit into holes in the tabletop. When the tabletop is 2 or so inches thick, or when a thick cleat has been fastened to the underside of the top and the hole for the leg drilled through cleat and top, the resultant joint is fairly strong. However, at best, this type of joint is never as strong as the leg-to-apron joint. And when the tabletop is less than 2 inches thick the joint is weak indeed. Side pressure on the leg can loosen it fairly easily. Such legs should always be braced by stretchers.

Metal legs may be fastened to wood and composition tabletops by bending the end of the leg and drilling holes through it. Then screws are slipped through the holes and driven into the wood. This type of joint is very weak. A moderately heavy side push on the leg will rip out the screws. Better joints are made by

A sturdy, unpainted hardwood table can serve in the kitchen for both working and eating. This one accommodates boards for extra length, and has a stout pedestal so there are no table legs to hamper the sitters.

welding metal plates to the top ends of the legs. These plates are then screw-fastened to the underside of the tabletop. This method produces strong joints when the metal plate is at least 3 or more inches in each direction. A variation consists of a metal plate with a pressure clamp that holds the end of the leg, allowing the leg to be removed for storage or moving. This type of joint is also very strong if the plate is fairly large and the clamp engages at least 2 inches of leg end. If the clamp is of thin metal and skimpy, or if the plate is small, the metal-to-wood joint will be weak no matter how many screws may be used.

Wood or metal legs are never joined directly to glass or marble tabletops. Glass may rest upon a frame and remain in place of its own accord, but for safety it should be held in place either by a continuous or a semicontinuous edging. Unless the glass is very thick it should be supported at several points.

Marble tops are sometimes cemented to a wood support—actually the tabletop. The wood support does not have to reach all the way out to the edge of the marble, but no more than a foot or so of marble should extend beyond the support. If it does, the marble may easily be broken off. Some marble tops

View from underneath a chair with a well-made bottom. The corner brace is thick and solid and the screws are countersunk.

are not only supported on wood but enclosed in a wood border. This is the strongest form of support and visually more interesting because of the contrast between the wood edging and the marble.

Trestle tables. These deserve a few words of their own because the bracing on these tables is deceptive; they may appear to be strongly braced when actually they are not.

A trestle table consists of a top supported by two legs. The legs are made of wide boards and face each other, so that when a brace is fastened from board to board, the legs and brace form the letter H. The width of the brace is relatively unimportant. It is its height, or vertical thickness, that counts. This dimension should be at least 10% of the distance between the table legs. For example, on a 60-inch-long table, with legs about 40 inches apart, the height (vertical width) of the brace should be 4 inches or more.

When the height of this brace is much less, any force against the end of the table acts to rip the legs from the tabletop.

Some trestle tables have four legs, with each pair of legs fastened with a brace. To test the effectiveness of the leg brace, push against the end of the table. There should be no give; the legs should be firm.

Modern kitchen furniture for those with the luxury of lots of room: the chairs are of metal and plastic, easy to clean but uneconomical of space.

KITCHEN CHAIR SIZES AND DESIGNS

Designs. Size is closely tied to design; since the size of kitchen chairs must be restricted, the range of design is limited to two: the straight-backed chair and the arm, or captain's, chair. There are innumerable variations on these two themes, but the essential difference lies in the floor space they require. The armchair needs an easy 20% or more of floor space. The armchair is usually made broader and in some designs the arms swing outward a bit.

Straight-backed kitchen chairs can be purchased with seats as little as 14 inches wide and 14 inches deep. Armchairs usually start with bottoms 16 inches wide, and the seats are usually 15 or more inches deep.

One thing to bear in mind when you select your kitchen chairs is that unless the person sitting is bulky or heavy in the regions below the waist, the small-bottom chair is as comfortable as the larger, and in some instances even more comfortable, because if the backs of his or her knees hit the edge of the chair before their back hits the chair's back, they will not sit comfortably.

Also bear in mind when choosing between arm and armless kitchen chairs that not only do the armchairs need more floor space at the table, they need more when you move them out of the way.

Chair-seat heights vary from 17 to 18 inches from the floor to the top of the seat or the top of the pad, if there is one.

Kitchen and dining room table heights vary from 19 to 20 inches above the floor.

Construction material. Most kitchen chairs are made of wood, the hardwoods as always being the better choice. The harder the wood the better. This is easily checked; the heavier chairs are made of harder wood.

Some chairs are made of metal, usually from metal pipe bent into shape. There is nothing wrong with metal chairs, if you accept their appearance. Unless they are made of such thin or small-diameter pipe that they are easily bent, they will last as long as, or longer than, wood chairs. However, metal chairs are plated and the plating does wear through in time. When this happens the metal rusts—usually you see small specks of rust at first. There is no practical cure for this.

Naturally, the thicker the plating the longer it lasts. Unfortunately, there is no way we can measure or even judge the thickness of the chromium plating on metal furniture. To assume the most expensive metal furniture has the thicker plating is to place a lot of faith in manufacturers and their pricing methods.

Construction. Essentially, chairs are made like tables. Four legs have to be fastened to a flat surface: the seat. The better wooden chairs have generous aprons on three or four sides of the chair bottom. The legs are joined to the apron by mortise and tenon. The aprons are joined to the seat bottom with glue and screws. Less desirable chair legs are joined by dowel joints.

When there is no apron the legs must have stretchers. If not, the first time someone tilts back in the chair (and someone always does), the legs start to loosen.

Good stretchers are not square in cross section—they are wider in one dimension than in the others. A square stretcher almost invariably terminates in a dowel-shaped end, which fits into a circular hole in the leg. If someone steps on the stretcher it will then tend to turn underfoot, and to tear the joint loose. A stretcher with a rectangular cross section usually terminates in a mortise and tenon joint, which cannot be turned. Therefore the joint holds better and longer.

Finish. Everything that was said about varnish and paint on kitchen tabletops pertains to finishes on wooden chairs. The decorated painted chairs may look pretty at first, but the paint soon wears off and repainting is a troublesome task if you want a like-new appearance. Therefore, varnish is much easier to work with.

PADS AND PADDING

A pad is a cushion that can be positioned on a chair bottom or against its back. Generally, pads come with ties to hold them in place. The better pads have zippered covers that can be removed and washed. The better pads also have a second, non-removable covering over the inner rubber cushion. This second covering helps keep oil and grease away from the rubber and, most important, keeps out light. Light speeds the deterioration of rubber. Even if the pad is plastic foam, the inner cover helps.

Padding differs from pads in that it is permanently fastened in place. It differs from upholstery in that it covers one surface only, while upholstery covers several surfaces.

Padding material. Today, the most frequently used padding material is plastic foam made of urethane. While it will not last forever, it does resist sunlight and oil to a considerable degree.

Its bounce depends upon its density and thickness. The denser and heavier the pad the longer it will hold its shape. The thicker the pad the softer and springier the seat. However, thickness without density is almost worthless. To check, try sitting on it. If you can feel the supporting board beneath the padding, the pad is either too thin or too light.

The pad is held in place most frequently by plastic sheeting. Cloth would be prettier, but would soon be soiled. Plastic can be wiped clean.

Unfortunately, plastic becomes brittle with cold and age. When it cracks it is not always easily replaced. When seat back and bottom are boards held in place by screws, it is a simple matter to remove the screws and replace the plastic covering. But in the case of some metal chairs there is no practical way of removing backs and bottoms; they are integral with the chair frame. These chairs become worthless when the plastic sheeting covering the padding cracks.

COUNTER TOPS

Many of us do eat and enjoy our meals at a counter-top table in our home, so counter tops are part and parcel of furniture.

Top material. Since a counter top functions as a table, the same materials that are most desirable for a table are equally desirable for a counter top.

Dimensions. A counter top height of 32 to 36 inches is comfortable for most people. What is very important but frequently omitted from many counter top designs, is knee space. Without a knee space of at least 6 inches, no one is going to sit comfortably at the counter, and a few additional inches would be even better.

Stools. What was said about kitchen chairs also applies to counter-top stools, or "bar stools." No aprons are used with

The legs go right through the seat, the traditional way to construct a wooden stool. This is a strong joint when the stool seat is thick enough, but the stretchers are a must for long wear.

wooden stools, but metal stools sometimes have metal aprons. In a wooden stool the legs go through holes in the seat and are fastened that way. This makes for a weak stool. The old, and much better, stools solved this problem by reinforcing the legs with long thin bolts that pulled the legs together. If you can find a stool reinforced in this way, the extra cost will more than repay you in extended life.

The alternative is to reinforce the stool yourself with wire. This is easy to do, but the results are not attractive.

5

Dining Room Furniture

Unlike a kitchen or a breakfast nook, which in some homes may be used twenty-one times a week, few dining rooms are used even every evening. In many families the dining room is reserved for special occasions. Therefore, dining room furniture does not have to stand the same abuse as kitchen furniture.

Another important point of difference is the nature of dining. To dine comfortably means, among other things, more space on the table each individual can use. It also means more space between and around each diner. (Of course, much of this extra space is provided by the very size of a dining room as compared to a kitchen or breakfast alcove.) However, additional pieces of furniture must be considered from the point of view of the floor space and clearance they need, as well as their utility and appearance.

TABLE DIMENSIONS AND SHAPES

Dining room tabletop surfaces are usually 28 to 29½ inches above the floor. While this is not a critical dimension, you should stay clear of tables with tops much higher or lower. If such a table is offered, try sitting at it on the chair you plan to use. With lower than normal tables, the skirt or apron will often strike a tall sitter's knees. Higher than normal tables are uncomfortable for short people and children.

Eating space. Furniture designers generally allow a minimum of 22 inches of table width—elbow to elbow, you might say—for each individual. Table depth in front of each individual is generally at least 18 inches from the table's edge to its center. Thus, for example, at a minimum a dining table designed for four would be at least 44 inches long and 36 inches wide. These figures, as you can see, provide about ⅓ more table space for each individual than a breakfast table.

Put a ruler to an offered table and find out how many it will comfortably seat. When a salesperson says that a table will seat eight it doesn't mean they will be comfortable even if eight chairs come with it. It is best to measure.

End sitters. Naturally you can place chairs and people at the head and foot of a table, but there is one fact you should bear in mind. End-of-table eating spaces are not space efficient. If the table, for example, is 36 inches wide and seats guests face to face, the person at the table end still needs 18 inches or so of space in front. On the other hand, if you extend the table just 4 inches, you could seat two people, face to face, at its end. If you are short of room space, this is something worth keeping in mind. Also, the table is easier to service if there is no one sitting at its ends. The person serving can place and remove dishes much more easily with the table ends open.

Leaves. A table leaf is a board that is added to the middle of a table to make it longer. The tabletop is constructed in two halves mounted on some sort of slide mechanism. When the two halves are pulled apart, the leaf is inserted and the halves brought to press against it. Some tables have no provisions for a leaf. Some tables can accommodate a single leaf, some can handle two.

Generally, tables with leaves cost more than tables without them. It is not the cost of the boards alone, but the cost of the mechanism. But if you expect to entertain, it is wise to opt for a leaf table with two boards. The second board does not cost very much more.

If you do select a dining room table with leaves, be certain to try the table first and to fit the leaves in place. Do not accept the table or the leaves if the leaves are warped.

Inspect the slide mechanism carefully. It should be sturdy and operate smoothly. Inspect the boards to make certain they match the rest of the table. The better leaves have short, projecting dowels that engage the tabletop and help lock everything together.

Store the leaves on end in a dry place, otherwise they will warp in time.

Oval versus rectangular tables. Here the decision involves three factors: appearance, cost, and space efficiency. We can only provide firm advice on the last. The other two are a matter of your taste, the shape and size of the room, its windows and other furnishings, and how much more you care to spend for the table of your choice than for an almost-as-pleasing table.

Some people prefer rectangular tables, some prefer oval. Neither is more beautiful than the other; neither is more formal or less formal than the other. If you are lucky enough to have an

Round dining table with machine-carved apron. It opens up to accommodate two leaves.

A rectangular table with rounded corners is the best use of dining-room space. The breakfront combines the functions of a serving table, a storage place for linen and tableware, and a china closet.

oval dining room, the oval table is probably first choice. Most of us do not own oval dining rooms, but there are many homes with large oval-shaped bay windows. If such a window has a commanding position in the room an oval table is worth considering. At the same time you might also consider an oval rug to go with the table.

When the dining room has arched-top windows or drapes pulled back in graceful curves, an oval table is also worth considering. The same can be said about a large circular chandelier that will hang directly above the table.

If you already have the chairs and other dining room furniture and the shape of this furniture is curved or suggests curves, an oval table might be the better choice.

Now we come to cost. Most often, oval tables cost more than rectangular tables of equal surface area. Just how much more depends on too many factors to enumerate here.

There is a real difference in manufacturing cost. Obviously, to make an oval tabletop you first make it rectangular and then

A trestle table eliminates the conflict of diner's legs vs. the table's legs. Check that the stretcher is wide enough (vertically) to brace the table firmly.

cut away the corners. If the top is supported by an apron or skirt it must also be curved. Very often, the legs on an oval table will be curved as well.

When we come to space efficiency, we can be definite. Oval tables conserve some floor space because their corners are rounded. Just how important this may be depends on the size of your dining room, its proportions and what other furniture you plan to install.

An oval table that is broad at its midpoint provides space for centerpieces, food platters and the like, an advantage over a minimum-width rectangular dining room table.

TABLE MATERIALS AND CONSTRUCTION

Solids. Many dining room tables are still made of solid pieces of wood. These may be long pieces glued side by side, or they may be short pieces glued in square and rectangular patterns much like flooring. The better-made solid tables of long pieces usually have cross pieces of wood at the ends. These hide the end grain of the long boards and help lock these boards together. A less desirable method of manufacture consists of either gluing a strip of wood across the ends of the table or sealing the ends with paint to hide the grain.

Tabletops consisting of small pieces of solid wood usually have one continuous border of solid wood (with joints) circumscribing the tabletop.

In both cases the quality of the tabletop depends on the wood that is used and its thickness. The joints between the boards are unimportant to us for several reasons. First, they are now all machine-made, so they are as nearly perfect as possible. Second, we cannot tell from surface examination whether glue alone is used to join them or they are joined by splines, tongue-and-groove or even dowels or steel bolts. And usually the salesperson doesn't know. So the best we can do, if the manufacturer's literature doesn't tell us, is accept what we see. Of course, the top is stronger if more than just glue is used, but since we cannot find out, why chew on the question.

You can estimate tabletop thickness either by looking at the real edge of the table or estimating it by looking behind the false edge. Obviously the thicker it is, the better. Another method is to lift the table and see how heavy and solid it is. It should be heavy.

As to the kind of wood, the harder it is the better. You can test for pine and other softwoods by using a sharp-pointed instrument on the underside of the tabletop. The salesperson or the sales literature should also clearly indicate what wood is used. Incidentally, the last word in the description should be the actual species. Mahogany-stained hemlock is hemlock, not mahogany.

The heft or weight of the table will also give you some clue as to the hardness of the wood. The harder woods are heavier.

Now, some of the hardwoods and many of the softwoods are stained to make them look more attractive or more like other, more desirable woods. There is nothing wrong with wood stains per se; they are no more likely to change than the wood color itself. However, sometime in the future that top is going to need refinishing. When it does, the fact that it was stained will make the refinishing more difficult. When the top is sanded down, its color will become uneven, because stain never penetrates equally through all portions of a piece of wood.

Veneer. Since a dining room table is not used very often and then, we presume, with care, the major objection to a veneer tabletop doesn't apply. With care, a veneer top will last for many, many years.

When you broaden your field of choice to include veneer, almost any wood surface becomes financially feasible. In addition, you then also have a choice of figuring—grain pattern—and marquetry—patterns and even pictures produced by using a number of different pieces of veneer. Obviously, the more complex the marquetry, the more costly the table.

This is a point worth considering: Is the beauty of intricate marquetry worth the additional cost? Will the marquetry be visible to your guests, or do you always use a tablecloth? If you do, the marquetry is only on show when you are not dining.

One more caution. The more intricate the marquetry the more easily it is damaged by spilled hot liquid and the more difficult and costly it will be to repair, because the individual pieces are smaller and more numerous.

Note that table legs are never covered with veneer. They are usually glazed, which means that they are given a thin coat of paint and then varnished to match the top color. Table aprons are sometimes veneered and sometimes not. In our opinion, better not, from the point of view of durability. It is too easily loosened.

Top protection. Years ago, sheets of plate glass were often used to protect the finish on dining room tabletops and other fine wood furniture. The glass does not rest directly on the wood but is separated from it by thin circles of cork placed here and there.

Glass is an excellent protective material, but it has some disadvantages you should consider. First, there is its cost. A large sheet of plate glass is not inexpensive. Then there is the task of removing it from the tabletop. If the glass is larger than

5 feet by 3 feet two people are needed to move it safely. Now that you have removed it, where are you going to put it? In a modest-sized apartment this can be an insurmountable problem.

Pads are another surface protection often used. These are ½-inch or thicker pads of firm material available at furniture stores. They are placed under a tablecloth when the table is in use.

TABLE CONSTRUCTION

From the point of view of appearance, one considers shape, size, wood type, color, shape of the legs and the design and width of the apron. From the point of view of construction, the joinery between the legs and the tabletop is most important, with the use of stretchers and their joinery secondary. Little else (except for the mechanism of an expandable table) has any bearing on table construction.

A well-constructed table has strong top-to-leg joints. Just how this strength is provided is relatively unimportant. However, certain construction methods naturally produce stronger joints.

Apron joints. The most common method and in some ways the strongest, consists of using an apron, which is a series of boards, positioned on end horizontally beneath the top of the table.

These boards should be ¾-inch thick or more, at least 3 inches wide (high) and fastened to the underside of the tabletop by means of glue, glue blocks, and screws. Glue blocks alone are not enough. If there are screws used, you will see them.

The legs can be joined to the apron in any of several ways. The most commonly used method today is by means of hanger bolts. The top of the leg is cut so that it locks against the underside of the table and the side of the apron. The bolt goes through the apron and into the leg. A nut on the bolt holds it in place. Properly made, there is no load or pressure on the bolt itself. The bolt just holds the leg in place. The advantage of this method is that the table legs can be removed for transportation and storage.

To check on whether or not this joint is properly made, loosen the nut a little. Even with the nut loose the leg should remain in place and be fairly stable. If loosening the nut causes the table to begin to collapse, the bolt is doing all the holding and the joint is not well designed and constructed.

Legs are also joined to aprons by mortise and tenon joints or dowel joints. Tenon joints are much stronger and preferred. There is no way of determining which is which after the joint has been assembled, but, usually when the surface of the leg projects beyond the front surface of the apron by ½ inch or so the joint is a mortise and tenon joint.

How important is all this?

Well, if we had a choice of two tables that were otherwise identical, we'd opt for the table with properly bolted legs, or at least the table that appeared to have mortise and tenon joints. On the other hand if one table had everything we wanted but its legs were probably fastened with dowels and the joints looked good, we would choose that. If a table is excellent except that the legs and apron are obviously held in place by nothing more than glue blocks and glue and possibly a poorly designed hanger bolt support, we would pass it up.

Trestle tables. The facing legs or pairs of legs on a trestle table may be fastened to the tabletop in any number of ways. One of the best is by means of a sturdy steel bracket that is screwed fast to the underside of the tabletop and either bolted or fastened by screws to the top ends of the legs. In some cases you can remove the screws or bolts and take the table apart for transportation or storage.

Another method utilizes a thick wood cleat fastened to the underside of the table. The leg or legs are bolted or screw-fastened to the side of the cleat.

Neither the bracket nor especially the cleat method of fastening can go it alone. The facing legs must be braced. This is done with a thick stretcher running from one leg or pair of legs to the other. (It can and often is a wide board on edge.) It is this height that provides the bracing action. Doubtful? Push endways on the table. If it swings to any noticeable degree, it is not properly braced.

Pedestal tables. Kitchen and casual pedestal tables have a single central leg terminating in some kind of base. Dining room pedestal tables may have two legs terminating in a long, wide base or a single enormously thick leg and base.

The pedestal table eliminates the nuisance of table legs, which often get in the way of the diners. But the base will never provide as shakefree a support as legs will.

The base presents other problems; it collects dust and some guests place their feet on it, marring its finish.

CHAIRS

Like kitchen chairs, dining room chairs are primarily divided into two designs: straight and armchairs. And like kitchen chairs, the same basic reason for selecting one design over another exists. However, most people prefer side (armless) chairs in the dining room. When you see armchairs in a dining room, you generally see no more than two, which were part of the package deal that went to make up the "set." Why manufacturers and dealers should adhere to the belief that everyone wants at least two armchairs in their dining room is beyond us. This is your basic decision. Bear in mind that armchairs take up more space and the arms are usually a pain when you are dining.

Padding. Pads are merely cushions that are tied in place. They have the advantage of easy removal and cleaning, if you purchase either washable pads or pads with zippered covers.

While many people believe that dining room chairs with pads are not quite formal, there is no reason you cannot remove the pads when you want to be ultra formal. All dining room chairs are not padded by any means.

"Padding" is pads held in place permanently by some type of fabric or material. You avoid the nuisance of tying and untying pads. To many, the chairs look more elegant. But the covering material can become soiled. So here we go, another decision. Shall we select padding covers of cloth or of leather or one of the many good imitation leathers currently on the market?

This decision is a matter of taste and overall room styling. If the furniture is to be dark and heavy, with a Spanish motif for example, then leather is excellent. If the furniture is light, graceful, as the French antique style, cloth is called for, possibly a brocade with a design reflecting the period.

The "hardness" of the cloth you select—the tightness of the weave—affects its soil resistance and wearability. Brocade, for example, stands up to wear and soil much better than velvet.

In most cases it will be easy to recognize the difference in soil and wear resistance between two upholstery fabrics. And the upholsterer who does the work should be able to point out the difference. When the appearance of two fabrics is relatively the same, the synthetic, or the fabric with the greatest percentage of synthetic fibers, is generally most resistant.

Soil guards. There are a number of compounds on the market which to some degree reduce the tendency of fabric to soil and absorb water. These protective compounds are best applied by the mill. You can also purchase them in spray cans and apply them yourself. If you do so, test the compound first on an unseen corner of the fabric.

Color. (In this case the color of the padding.) In our opinion it is wise to eschew the bright colors—the reds and grass greens and oranges so often seen in color photographs in magazines. We do not believe that you can live with them. In a short time, for example, the bright red imitation leather padding on dining room chairs will become annoying.

We suggest you choose a padding color that complements the color of the furniture and the overall style of the room. Again, if it is a dark and moody Spanish atmosphere you are seeking, very dark, almost black leather or imitation leather padding supplements the feeling. A medium brown might go well with American Colonial or French Provincial. But in our opinion, in no instance should the padding be the most striking color in the room.

Color belongs in every room; as an interesting oil painting or two on a pale wall; as a flower centerpiece on the dining room table; as the reflection of sunlight on the furniture and walls, but not in overwhelming power and mass.

Type of padding. Again, a decision may be called for. There are basically two types. One consists of padding material on a board. The fabric or leather is placed over the padding and nailed to the underside of the board. Then the board is fastened to the chair.

The advantage of this arrangement is twofold. The board and its covering is simple and easy to remove. Almost anyone willing to make the effort can re-cover the boards. The other is that the edges of the upholstered boards are usually below the surface of the seat's edges; thus, the edges of the upholstery are somewhat protected from wear. Since the edges usually wear first, this is important.

The other design consists of a permanent chair seat and back, padding fastened to them, and fabric or leather nailed in place along the sides or rear of the chair. (You will have no trouble recognizing the two designs.) The advantage here is visual. More fabric is used and since the fabric goes over the edges of the chair, the visual effect is one of rounding. Chairs upholstered or padded in this way appear to be softer and more comfortable.

It is not too difficult to reupholster chairs padded by the second method, but it is more difficult than the first. You have to draw the fabric smoothly over the corners; tack it carefully in place and very often you have to cover the tacks with a trim of some kind. Still, it is not beyond the skills of the average home craftsman. The disadvantage of the second type is that it has a much higher rate of wear.

Naturally, if you have the work done, the second type will cost much more than the first.

Design. Although there must be thousands of different chair designs, selection is not at all difficult. If you purchase a dining room set the manufacturer furnishes chairs that match the rest of the furniture in the set. If you select chairs to complement a particular table, the table itself dictates the color, wood, and design of the chairs.

If you have a table at home and go shopping for chairs, bring along a color photograph of the table, even if you have to rent an instant camera for it. The ability to match a color from memory is rarer than perfect pitch. With photo in hand, you can easily select chairs that complement your table. Work by memory and you will deceive yourself.

For a complementary color match you need to have the same tone, or close to it. So long as you are dealing with different degrees of saturation of the *same* color, they all blend well. But even a slightly different color no longer blends.

When possible you should stick with the same wood. When this is not possible, do what we all do—compromise.

The other side of the decorating coin is contrast. Some people prefer that there be contrast in color and even in wood and texture between table and chairs. If this is your taste, fine. But if you do elect to have the colors contrast, do not have the styles contrast as well. If the table is a heavy, dark-stained oak piece in the style of a refectory table, for example, you certainly would not select light-wood Swedish Modern chairs to accompany it.

Unless you have made yourself an expert, don't try to match chairs to tables by major period or design descriptions. For example, unless you know that the table is Federalist, don't run about seeking Federalist chairs. Not that it is impossible, it is just very expensive. Simply select chairs with overall shapes and proportions that look well with your table, or vice versa.

In addition to comparing the chairs you are considering to your table, keep in mind the overall design of your dining room.

A very formal room would favor straight-backed chairs with
flat backs. An informal room would look better with chairs having lower backs with some curve in their design.

Construction. Except for what has been discussed, the
same rules suggested for selecting kitchen chairs apply to dining
room chairs. The heavy hardwood chairs with stretchers are
strongest.

SIDEBOARDS, BUFFETS, AND SERVING TABLES

Sideboard and *buffet* are interchangeable terms. They
denote a long cabinet with one or more swing doors, supported
by legs and designed to be backed up against a wall. The top of
the sideboard is usually 32 to 35 inches high, 20 or so inches
deep and 50 or more inches long.

A small sideboard is called a serving or service table. Again
it is a cabinet with one or more swing doors, supported by legs.
Its top is about the same height as its big brother, but generally
it is shallower, perhaps 16 to 18 inches deep and only 35 or so
inches long.

Both the sideboard and the serving table may have one
drawer above the swing door or doors. This drawer is used for
silver and other flatware. The space behind the swing doors is
used for linens, chafing dishes, ordinary dishes, and other
equipment useful in the dining room.

Sideboards that do not have swing doors are really chests of
drawers. They can be used in dining rooms, and they can look in
place and attractive there. However, the utility of a chest of
drawers is limited to linen and flatware. One cannot fit large
objects like punch bowls and chafing dishes into a chest of
drawers. Still, some salespeople will attempt to sell you one,
calling it a sideboard or buffet. It isn't. If you have large
platters and the like, you will not be able to store them in a chest
of drawers.

In addition to storage, sideboards have an active utilitarian
purpose. They can save anyone serving at meals miles of walk-

ing. You can put anything not immediately required on the sideboard. This is where your chafing dishes can stay and your electric percolator can chug along until coffee is needed. And, of course, you can serve a buffet meal from the top of your buffet.

When the dining room is small, sideboards are sometimes placed in an adjoining living room. There they can be used almost as conveniently as if they were inside the dining room. More often, they serve mainly to enhance the living room, rather than as useful ancillary dining room furniture.

Space requirements. Sideboards absorb little more space than the floor they stand on. While they do have doors that swing wide, these doors are kept closed, so they do not interfere with traffic. However, you do have to take into account their depth when they are positioned alongside doorways and other lanes of traffic.

Choice of designs. The overall design of one sideboard does not differ greatly from another. Some designs have one or two drawers running the width of the piece just under the top. There are designs with one, two, and three doors, depending on length, and there are designs with short legs and long legs. The height of the legs is important only in that short-legged sideboards have more storage space, but are difficult to clean underneath. Some sideboards have a carved front and legs, others do not.

Choice of design is primarily dictated by your choice of table and chairs, assuming you have selected them first. The table, being the largest single piece, is dominant and more or less establishes the overall feeling of the room. However, since the sideboard is a distance away from the table, there does not have to be as close a match in design between the sideboard and table as between the chairs and the table. There should, of course, be some overall tone between the sideboard and the table. An exact duplication, as you may find in a "set," is unnecessary, though not at all undesirable.

On the other hand, too great a dissimilarity will definitely look poor. You will not like the result, for example, of placing an early-20th-century sideboard of natural oak in the same room with light, airy and graceful French Provincial table and chairs, especially if the latter have a painted finish decorated with hand-painted flowers. The same sideboard *would* look good with an oak trestle table and bare oak chairs, even though a trestle table is basically "rustic" in style. But if one piece has been stained a dark shade of brown and the other left light-colored and natural, they won't look good together.

Very simply the pieces have to feel "right" together. They do not have to be cut from the same tree or even to exactly the same design.

There is one exception, however. If the sideboard is authentically antique, it will almost always "go" no matter how great the visual disparity. The antique is a "display" piece. No one expects it to belong visually. It is a treasure and complete in itself.

Construction. Most often the sideboard and the serving table have four legs that reach to the underside of the top. All the other parts tie into these legs. Therefore the legs, which also form the corners of the piece, must be substantial. We cannot give you specific minimum dimensions, since a sideboard with legs a fraction under any arbitrary figures would still be acceptable, but you should examine them carefully. They must have heft, "visual strength." This may sound vague, but if you examine a number of sideboards of various design and price you will quickly see what we mean.

Some designs are not as described above. The pieces have separate, short legs fastened beneath the *body* of the sideboard. This arrangement introduces a weakness. We would not completely disqualify a piece made in this way, but we would certainly subtract a few points from its overall evaluation.

The same guidelines suggested for tabletops apply also to the top of the sideboard. It does serve as a table, and to some extent may be abused as much as a kitchen table. If you are planning to use the sideboard for chafing dishes, electric coffee-makers and the like, you would be well advised to select a solid top, certainly one that is close to an inch thick.

See that the doors are also substantial, that the hinges are mortised in place, that the fit between doors and cabinet is good, that the doors are flat and not warped, and that the latch mechanism works smoothly.

See that the inside of the cabinet is smoothly finished, with no rough spots, or protruding nails or screws. See that there are a number of adjustable and removable shelves within the cabinet, that they are flat and not warped, that the shelves are varnished so that they cannot absorb moisture, which would cause them to warp.

Special devices and gadgets within the cabinet such as glass holders, wine bottle racks, etc., are extras that are not essential. Don't let these confections blind you to the true value of the piece. If this is the sideboard of your choice and it has internal extras, splendid; but don't purchase any sideboard on the basis of the extras.

The sides, back, and bottom of sideboards are almost always made of plywood. (Unless you are dealing with an antique.) This is of less than secondary importance. The back and bottom are never seen. The sides have a veneer matching the balance of the furniture. However, the plywood under it should be at least ¼ inch thick, and the veneer should be attractive, unless the entire piece is painted. To save money some manufacturers "paint" the sides of their sideboards even though fronts and tops may be varnished. Recognize these pieces for what they are—borax (junk). And some manufacturers make sides, bottoms, and backs from plywood so thin you can push it in, almost, with your fingers. Test for plywood thickness by rapping the sides with your knuckles.

Drawers on sideboards should slide in and out smoothly. Even very long drawers should not "cock"—slide at an angle and so get stuck. Each drawer should have at the minimum one central guide, a board or pair of boards that help keep the drawer from cocking. Remove the drawer and examine it. That will expose the guide or guides, if there are any.

A good drawer is made from hardwood. The bottom may be of plywood; it should be flat and not warped. The sides, back and front of the drawer should be held together by joints. These are readily visible when the drawer is removed. A drawer held together by nails and glue is a drawer that will soon come apart.

Now we return to heft. All things being equal, the heavier sideboard has the greater quantity of wood and/or its wood is harder and heavier. The more wood used and the harder the wood, the better its construction (generally but not always) and the stronger the piece of furniture. When you go out shopping for a sideboard, lift an end. You will soon learn that there can be a tremendous difference in weights.

HUTCHES

You might describe a modern hutch as a kind of bookcase without doors. Instead it has strips of wood running across the front of each shelf to hold things in place. Often the strips of wood are scalloped, and sometimes there are vertical, decorative strips of wood at the sides of the shelves. The shelves do not extend down to the floor but rest on or are part of a sideboard, a serving table or a chest of drawers. Since the shelf or hutch portion of the furniture is not as deep as the supporting cabinet, some people call a hutch a breakfront.

Doesn't work as a buffet. Although the shelf portion of most hutches is not as deep as the top of the cabinet on which it rests, shelves overhang the top of the cabinet and the cabinet itself is not, generally, as deep as a sideboard. Hutches, therefore, are not satisfactory replacements for sideboards. They can be used but they offer limited storage and the feeling is one of "tightness."

Construction materials. Like sideboards, the back, bottoms and sides of a hutch are most often made of plywood. This is the least expensive material and entirely satisfactory if it is thick enough. When the front, top and shelves of the hutch are painted, the sides can also be painted. But when the rest of the hutch is finished in varnish, the sides should be also. Painted sides on an otherwise clear-finished hutch indicate a very low level of workmanship.

The front, top, and shelves of a hutch are usually made of solid wood. It is very difficult to veneer scalloped trim, and intricately figured veneer would not look in place on what is otherwise a simply ornamented piece of furniture. Scallops remind one of country carpenters, Amish and Pennsylvania Dutch styles. Very often the doors on a hutch's cabinet are ornamented with simple carvings or moldings fastened in place.

The top of the cabinet is, of course, flat. This could easily be veneered and some manufacturers do veneer this surface. Since the hutch's top will not be used for service often, the way one would use a sideboard, veneer is sufficiently strong here. However, we do not believe marquetry is appropriate for this surface.

Some tops will be made of plywood. This is quite satisfactory if the plywood is at least ¾ inch thick or more. Note that while the top surface of a sheet of plywood *is* a veneer, it is a large single sheet and stronger, usually, than the pieces used to veneer a table or similar surface.

Construction. The lower portion of a hutch is constructed much the same way as a sideboard. Essentially it is a cabinet. All the suggestions previously made for evaluating the construction of a sideboard can be applied to a hutch.

Now, some hutches are made to separate between the cabinet top and the bottom of the shelf portion. There is nothing wrong with this arrangement and it certainly makes transportation easier. But the top must do more than just sit there. There must be some locking action provided. Since this can be done in a dozen different ways, we cannot suggest one that is best. They are all good if made properly. You will just have to use your judgment here, but do make certain to examine the fastening. Just looking at the assembled piece will not tell you anything.

When you examine the shelves, look at the way the shelves are fastened to the vertical end pieces. There should be no open spaces or cracks. The joints should be invisible and tight. There should be no spaces between the rear of the shelves and the backboard. This board should be flat and unwarped. The scalloped trim in front should lie flat without spaces between it and the shelves. The edges of the trim should be smooth.

The paint and/or varnish inside the shelf portion of the hutch should be even and reach into all the corners. Bare spots indicate sloppy workmanship, and that should lead you to a more careful inspection of everything else.

Corner hutches. These are hutches shaped to fit into the corner of a room. The upper portion may have two or three shelves, the lower portion may have a drawer and one or two swing doors. On medium- and lower-priced corner hutches, the drawer will not work too well. It will cock. Note that the corner hutch does not go all the way into any corner, because the floor trim holds it out slightly. And sometimes the corner of your room is not perfectly square; don't hold that against the furniture maker.

Corner hutches usually have side scallops but no scallops in front of each shelf. Rear side panels are usually of plywood and fairly thin. This is not too important, as the panels are not large, but the side and rear posts should be sturdy.

All suggestions previously made in regard to sideboards and full-size hutches apply to corner hutches.

CHINA CABINETS

A china cabinet or closet is usually supported by short legs, almost always taller than it is wide, and designed to display the contents. It is rarely, if ever used to store a large number of dishes.

It may have glass doors set in wood frames, flat or curved glass sides, even a glass back. Some of the very old designs had mirror backs. Modern designs often utilize metal screens in place of the glass. When the metal is gilded and the wood dark, the combination is attractive. However, the screen allows dust and soil to enter and the screen itself soon tarnishes, even when it is covered with a thin layer of gold.

Where does it really belong? This is not as strange a question as it may seem at first. If beautiful dishes are displayed in a china cabinet, it would seem to belong in the dining room. And yet the dishes in a china closet are rarely removed. The entire cabinet is too fragile at best and the dishes too easily knocked about and damaged. So in a sense it is an exhibit piece. Does it look right in a dining room?

We believe the question can only be answered on an individual basis. We know that up until the 1930s, china closets were stuffed into dining rooms whether or not there was walking space around them. A china closet belongs where there is sufficient space to allow it to stand apart from everything else. It adds interest to a room but is not integral. By the same reasoning, we believe that a china closet would not be out of place in a library if something other than china were placed in it.

Then, do you need a china closet to complete a dining room? We do not believe so. If you are really pressed for space it is better to forgo it rather than have to slither around it going to and from your seat.

If you do have a large dining room or have one with a jog in the wall or an alcove, and you do have beautiful things to display or hope eventually to have them, a china closet may appreciably add to the beauty and interest of your room.

If you already have a china closet or many beautiful things to display, think of placing the china closet in your living room. The Victorians did it; their living rooms and often their libraries and day rooms looked like museums.

Construction materials. Years ago a lot of veneer was used in the making of china closets. This was not easy since in those halcyon days the closets had lots of glass and very thin wood frames supporting the glass. Many early-1900s china closets were made in this way. This is unfortunate because some china closets of this period were not properly cared for. Moisture got at the veneer and bits of it have been lost. It is not particularly difficult to replace the missing veneer, but it is hard to find veneer that matches well.

Today, the frames that support the glass are generally much wider. Little if any veneer is used. Most, if not all, the framework is solid lumber, and since lots of strength is needed, most of today's china cabinets are made of one hardwood or another. Comparatively low-priced china cabinets without glass, or even with glass whose frames are 3 and more inches wide and painted, may be of a softwood. (You can test the hardness of the wood with a pointed instrument on a hidden corner.) If the cabinet is otherwise satisfactory and attractive, the use of a softwood is not important. China cabinets do no more than stand silently in place. They do not suffer the wear and tear of other furniture. Unless you dust like a veritable fiend, the finish should last for generations.

Construction. A china closet is essentially a vertical box or cabinet resting on legs. For strength, the best design consists of corner posts that reach from the floor to the top of the cabinet. But many designs utilize short, curved legs fastened to the bottom of the cabinet. If this is the design on the cabinet you are evaluating, look underneath. See whether or not there are wood screws fastening the legs in place. Glue and nails alone are not enough. See that there is heft or body to the joint and that the top of the leg is not simply screwed into the bottom of the cabinet the way some coffee-table legs screw into the tabletop. See that the bottom of the cabinet is reasonably thick and not a thin board. Again we return to that vague but useful description, heft, meaning mass, a feeling of solidity and strength. The joints between the legs of the cabinet and the bottom and corner posts must have heft.

Now, no matter how thin and weak the cabinet may be, it will still support a *vertical* ton or more. So, if some fat salesperson offers to demonstrate the strength of a cabinet by climbing on top, let them. They need the exercise. But pay no attention to their claims. All cabinets can carry a vertical load, the test comes when the cabinet is tilted and the weight presses against the side of the legs. Weak legs will break off. Naturally one doesn't very often tilt china closets, but it does occur when moving furniture from place to place in one's home, and furniture movers have been known to pick up cabinets by their legs.

Examine the doors, their hinges, and the locks or latches. The doors must be perfectly flat and fit perfectly. Do not accept any cabinet with warped doors. They will not straighten out by themselves. Most likely the warpage will grow worse with age.

Shelves should be adjustable. They may be of glass or wood. If wood, plywood is better than a solid here as the plywood is less likely to warp.

6

Living Room Furniture

In previous chapters we discussed what might be termed "hard" furniture. Traditionally, living rooms are furnished with "soft" or upholstered, furniture.

A FEW TERMS

Upholstery means permanent padding of any kind on a seat or bench. When the term is used alone, it means that some of the wood frame is visible, other than the legs or lower ends of the legs. "Overstuffed furniture" or "overstuffed upholstery" means that none of the wood is visible, except possibly the lower ends of the legs. All else may be the same; it may even be the same frame style and size. If the upholstery hides the wood or metal, it is overstuffed.

The terms *sofa* and *couch* are interchangeable; both are forms of upholstered benches that can accommodate three or more people. A love seat is a sofa or couch that seats two. A settee is a couch or sofa with arms but no back. Its original purpose was as a daybed where one could nap.

Sectional furniture is two or more units that can be used individually as chairs or grouped to form a couch.

A Chesterfield is a type of couch. "Tuxedo" is a style with straight backs and straight arms as high as the backs. "Lawson" differs in that the arms are lower than the back.

Buttoned or tufted upholstery means that the surface of the chair or couch that the sitter's body comes in contact with has

"Upholstered" furniture like this sofa has permanent padding.

been indented in a number of places. This is done with buttons positioned on the surface of the upholstery and pulled down or back with strings. In some designs several buttons are installed in a horizontal line across the back of the chair. In others the buttons are positioned so as to form squares and diamonds.

Tufting is used to make an otherwise dull textile or plastic surface more interesting and to permit air to filter between the sitter and the settee.

Nontailored or draped upholstery is exactly what the words describe. The upholstery fabric is not cut, sewn, and tailored to fit over the padding and springs. Instead, it is draped over the padding. Its appearance is exactly the same as though you had placed fabric over the arm of a chair, for example, and gathered the ends together. Draped upholstery has lots of creases, overlapping folds and wrinkles. Its surface is soft, yielding, undulating. Since this type of upholstery requires but a fraction of the labor necessary for tailored upholstery, its price should be considerably less. Generally, draped upholstery is only used with plastic fabrics and plastic "leathers."

Tuxedo style sofa (the arms are the same height as the back) is "overstuffed"; there is no bare wood showing. (Furniture with just the ends of legs bare is also considered overstuffed.)

This sectional group has draped upholstery, easily identifiable by its loose folds.

BUYING PROBLEMS

A purchaser faces difficulties in evaluating soft furniture. Unlike hard furniture, where the top, bottom, inside and outside are completely visible, the construction of soft furniture is hidden. And unless a manufacturer is wise and particularly proud of his product, he does not exhibit cut-away examples of his furniture. Thus most of our evaluation in the case of soft goods must be made by surface inspection and touch alone. Compounding this handicap is the fact that roughly 25% of the cost of manufacturing upholstered furniture lies in the upholstery material itself.

The material is, of course, eminently visible. But making a reasonably accurate judgment of the fabric is more difficult than judging wood. While there are only a dozen or so woods commonly used for furniture today, there are hundreds of textile upholstery fabrics and weaves. In addition, fabrics are very expensive. A couch, for example, usually costs more than a dining room table. Which means the penalty for error is high.

Proof of this unsavory pudding lies in consumer complaint reports. While the greatest number of complaints are about excessive delays in deliveries and the delivery of scratched and otherwise damaged new furniture, next in frequency are complaints concerning fabrics that rip, soil, and wear out too quickly.

The answer, of course, is that you must be prepared to do a considerable amount of looking and pricing when you go to purchase soft furniture. And you should not buy until you are reasonably certain of what you are buying and that the price is fair.

SIZE

In addition to selecting a piece of furniture of a size that suits you and making certain it can be brought into your home, it is important to check seat dimensions for comfort.

Seat depth as measured from the front edge of the seat to

the chair or sofa back or cushion should be a minimum of 16 inches and a maximum of 20 inches. Some flashy but cheap sofas and chairs have a much greater depth of seat. This gives a luxurious appearance but is very uncomfortable to sit on. One's back cannot reach the furniture back. Sofa backs should measure at least 13 inches above the seat itself. A lower back does not provide adequate support and is uncomfortable.

FRAME MATERIALS AND CONSTRUCTION

Metal. Generally you will find metal frame furniture upholstered in drapery style and designed for use in a playroom, den, or other casual room or office.

Properly constructed, metal frames can last almost forever. So far as evaluation goes, all you can do is try to see just how firm the frame is by sitting on the furniture and pushing against its arms and back. Obviously, if it gives under your pressure, it is not too strong. This examination can only tell you if the piece is rather weakly made.

What is important is the gauge (thickness) of the pipe and other metal used, the thickness of the chrome plating, and whether or not the welded joints have been "relieved," which means they have been heated after welding to make them less brittle. The last is probably the most important step in making a welded frame. But even if you could examine the metal, all you could really see was whether or not it was thick or thin.

Weight is of some help when you are choosing between two pieces of equal size. Then you can safely assume the heavier is the stronger. Other than this rough guide, you have nothing to depend upon other than the manufacturer's reputation and that of the stores.

Wood. Generally, nothing but hardwoods are used for upholstered furniture frames. The portion of the frame that is visible is always sandpapered and varnished, and possibly also stained. Sometimes the exposed wood is carved. Softwood would not take stain as well and takes carving very poorly.

A cut-away view of a well-made sofa, showing frame, springing, padding and upholstery. This kind of demonstration piece is a great help to buyers, who in most cases cannot know much about what is under the top fabric.

Another reason for using hardwood is that in many designs the frame needs to be fairly thin in places, and softwoods would not stand up to the strain.

Since hardwood frame joints are almost always made by machine, they are strong. With a machine it is easy to make joints with complex mating surfaces that provide as much and even more strength than joints made with screws. So joints in upholstered furniture frames are neither a problem nor a concern.

Hardwood frames *do* tend to crack, so look for real and incipient cracks in the frame. In particular look closely at the sides where the frame makes a large curve. Where the grain goes directly across the width of the wood, as it often does at this portion of the frame, cracks are likely to appear and can be most damaging. A crack that runs lengthwise with the board can also separate the frame, but it usually does not traverse the entire length of the wood; even if it does, it is easily repaired.

Carving. Many frames are carved to some degree. Most of the carving done today is done by machine. On the better furniture, machine carving is followed by hand touch-up to make the carving a bit uneven, as though it were done by hand. So far as beauty and longevity are concerned, there is no difference; carving done by machine equals that done by hand.

Unfortunately, everything that appears to be carving is not; it may be molded wood composition, glued and nailed in place. You can recognize such an appliqué by its symmetrical edge and by the absence of grain. Applied carvings can break loose and fall off. Ornamentation carved into the wood will not.

Overstuffed frames. Since only the leg ends (and sometimes not even they) are visible on overstuffed furniture, softwood is used for most of this furniture today. There is plenty of room on the better grades for pieces of wood sufficiently thick for the job.

Unfortunately, a well-made overstuffed couch or chair has a dustcover over its bottom. Unless you are prepared to remove the tacks, there is nothing of the frame visible beyond the leg ends. However, you can recognize a well-made frame by its back legs. They should be continuous, from the floor to the top of the piece. You can feel this by running your hand up the outside corners.

The front legs are fastened to the frame that holds the springs and the rest of the seat assembly. They should be firmly fastened. You should not be able to turn these legs in your hand. If you can, they are fastened by a single, central screw, which is far from the best way to join the leg to its frame.

SPRINGING AND PADDING

Coil springs. The furniture maker starts with an open-bottom frame. He stretches bands of webbing made of strong, woven cloth about 3 inches wide across the lower side of the frame. The ends of the webbing are fastened to the wood with tacks. Coil springs are now placed on top of the webbing and held in place by strong string that locks the springs in place. On better furniture, eight pieces of string are used on each spring. Steel bands are sometimes used in place of webbing.

On some designs a stiff but flexible wire is used to outline the desired shape of the top of the spring support. The wire is fastened to the springs it touches. In some designs the springs are prefastened to this wire.

The springs are then covered with a layer of burlap. This is followed by some kind of padding or filler. The filler on better furniture is covered with white muslin or a similar cloth. The muslin is then covered with whatever upholstery fabric is used. Note that the muslin defines the final shape of the furniture. In the more expensive shops, the furniture is displayed in muslin and the buyer selects the final fabric.

No-sag springs. A steel wire is bent to resemble a series of waves, and a number of these springs are fastened side by side across the opening on the bottom of the seat or the back. Generally the springs are spaced about 2 or 3 inches apart. Sometimes one no-sag spring is joined to a neighbor by a smaller helical spring.

From here on, construction is almost identical with coil-spring construction. The no-sags are covered with a layer of some tough material, such as burlap, sometimes called "insulation." This is covered by padding or filler, followed by muslin and then the upholstery fabric.

Since the no-sag takes up much less space it permits "thinner" construction. That is why no-sag springing is used on the backs of almost all upholstered furniture. A coil-spring support needs a minimum of 5 or 6 inches. No-sag supports can do the job with as little as 2 inches.

Arch springs. The arch spring is a fairly recent innovation in the furniture industry. The springs are made of broad strips of spring steel curved into a shape that most resembles a flattened circle. The springs are fastened to the frame side by side; the resultant shape is somewhat similar to that of a cushion. The cushion of steel is then covered with a layer of insulation, which can be burlap, followed by a layer of padding, muslin, and finally the upholstery fabric.

Upholstering a sofa at Flexsteel Industries, one of the country's leading manufacturers of high-quality furniture. The arch-shaped blue steel springs are being attached to the hardwood frame.

The result is a firm, resilient seat just as comfortable as those made with other types of springs. Since there are no tie-cords to wear through, it would appear that this new type of springing can last as long as or longer than coil springs.

Springless. It is possible to provide a comfortable seat without springs. This is accomplished by using a very thick pad in place of the springs. The pad rests on a solid, wood support.

Arm padding. To secure a rounded, padded look on the arms of upholstered furniture, the wood frame is covered with a thick pad, sometimes shaped to accentuate the curve. The padding is covered with burlap, which in turn is covered by muslin and then the upholstery fabric.

APPLYING THE MUSLIN AND UPHOLSTERY FABRIC

With draped upholstery, the material is fastened at one end of the piece, pulled over the arm or back, tucked under and fastened there. No effort is made to secure a neat fit.

Both the muslin and the covering fabric of fitted upholstery have to be cut and sewn prior to application, much like a suit of clothes. This is highly skilled, time-consuming work. The

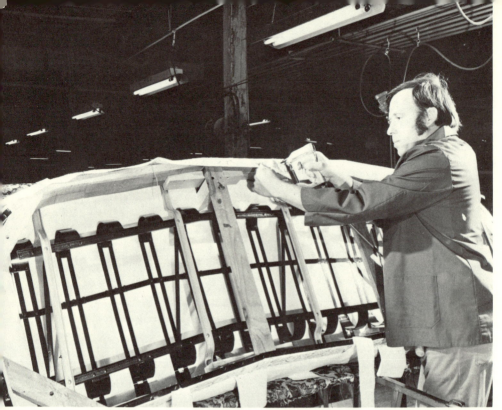

The next steps show the worker attaching the upholstery coverings to the frame.

fabric is tacked at one end, pulled smooth and tacked at the other. In some designs the tacks have large brass heads and are displayed. In others the tacking is done on the underside or the tacks are covered by a trim called gimp.

Some upholstery is merely sewn together to form a corner, other upholstery is sewn over a cord into a welt. Welts look neat and help to delineate the edges visually, but wear is greatest at the welt itself, and very often the welt will look worn before the rest of the fabric shows wear.

The final step consists of tacking a dustcover over the bottom and sometimes the back of the furniture.

EVALUATION

This is the hard part. It is not easy to recognize small differences in the quality of otherwise similar pieces of furniture. But if you follow our suggestions and spend sufficient time going from store to store, looking at many pieces of furniture, you will soon be able to tell at a glance.

We have described how to arrive at a rough measure of the quality of upholstered and overstuffed frames. Here is how you may measure the relative quality of the other construction.

Springing. Remove the seat and back cushions. Push down with your hand. Is there a smooth spring action? Are all the spring tops level with one another? There should be no obvious high or low spots.

Sit on the springs—without the cushion. Do you touch the bottom? You shouldn't. Your weight should not depress the springs so far that there is no more give.

Feel the metal edge beneath the padding forming the front edge. Is it straight, unbroken, and unbent? It should be. Look at the bottom and back of the piece. These surfaces should be reasonably flat, with just minor bumps. If there is a large bump, a web may be loose. If there is no dustcover, it is not top-quality furniture.

Padding. Remove the seat and back cushions. Feel the front edge of the seat or couch. It should be smoothly curved; firm, yet a little flexible. Feel the surface of the seat and back. Push down with your hand. You should feel a considerable thickness of padding beneath your hand. If there is nothing there but a single layer of cloth, the springs will soon work their way up through this.

Types of padding. Urethane foam is the most widely used padding material today. It is long lasting, rot- and mildew-proof. If it is thick enough and dense enough it will last a long, long time without compacting or flattening out under continuous use. There is no way you can check on the density of urethane foam padding already installed beyond testing it for "bottoming." Very simply, sit down heavily on the padding. If your weight compresses the foam sufficiently for your bottom to feel the seat, the padding is either too light, too thin, or both.

Next on the list of desirable padding materials is horse-hair, followed by pig's hair, which is not as good because it is straight. Years ago the hair was just stuffed into place. Today the hair is first dipped into rubber, which eliminates odor and helps keep the hairs from shifting.

Still lower on the list is moss, followed by kapok, another plant fiber. Then there is cotton and last and least desirable, excelsior. This is nothing more than fine, thin wood shavings. You are lucky if furniture with excelsior padding lasts more than a year or two.

Burlap with and without a backing of cotton padding is often used just above springs, to round off furniture edges. These pads are called rolls and are quite acceptable in places that do not need "bounce." They provide a firm, smooth base for a covering layer of muslin and the upholstery fabric.

Pillows. Pillows are filled with feathers, solid plastic foam, small pieces of foam, rubber, kapok, or cotton. The softest and the best pillows are filled with eider down, next is goose feathers, followed by chicken feathers. Prices are in the same order. Note that while down and feather pillows are softest, they are also the most easily compressed and have to be "fluffed" after anyone has been sitting on them.

Plastic foam solids are probably best when you want to avoid the bother of fluffing, and plastic foam pieces are probably next best. Rubber is almost as good as foam for cushions—some like it better. Kapok tends to pack down after a time and to break up into powder. Cotton will pack after repeated use and cannot be fluffed.

The best cushions are made with zipper covers so that the covers can be removed for cleaning. The filling or stuffing is best contained in heavy ticking.

United States law insists that all filler materials be listed on an attached tag. If you cannot find the tag, and the salesperson cannot find it for you either, beware.

Typically a tag may read: "All new material consisting of blended cotton felt 75%, the balance rubberized and curled

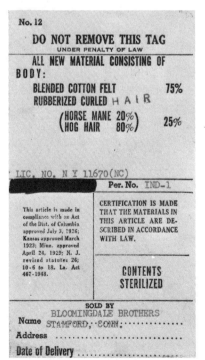

Typical tag listing the filler material in a sofa. It is required by U.S. law to be on all upholstered furniture, pillows and mattresses. Look for it.

hair. The hair being 20% horse mane, and 80% hog.'' A pillow tag may read: ''All new material. Gray duck down 25%; gray duck feathers 75%.

UPHOLSTERY FABRIC

We now enter an area in which countless people have spent their entire careers. There are literally thousands of different fabrics and hundreds of weaves. No one person knows it all. But for the selection of suitable upholstery, we really don't need to know very much at all.

Essentials. The synthetics, whatever their drawbacks, are stronger and longer lasting than the natural fibers. Price reflects manufacturing difficulty and material scarcity, and is only partly related to wear and soil resistance.

Synthetics. Some man-made fibers are better and more desirable than others.

Nylon is the toughest, hardest, and most resistant to wear. But it also generates the most static electricity when you slide across it, and it loses its color faster in sunlight than other synthetic fiber.

The vinyls are next in descending order of toughness. In addition to their strength, vinyls are not easily set afire. A dropped cigarette will most likely burn itself out safely.

Olefin is made of polyethylene and polypropylene. Not as tough as nylon and vinyl, it resists sunlight better than the other two. It also resists staining but once stained is much more difficult to clean. It is not easily ignited but does melt readily. Place a chair covered in olefin near an open fire, and it may melt while someone sits on it.

The polyesters tend to attract lint, are less resistant to wear than the fibers mentioned, and, while not easily ignited, will burn.

Rayon, while physically the weakest of all the synthetics, is used often. It combines well with the other synthetics, producing more lustrous colors, and resists the bleaching effect of sunlight very well.

Natural fibers. Today, some 40% of all upholstered furniture made is covered with cotton fabric. It is soft, takes colors very well, resists fading better than any other fiber and is relatively inexpensive. Unfortunately, it is physically weak, wears quickly, stains and soils easily, and is easily ignited.

Silk, on the other hand, is tough, stain resistant, fade resistant, highly lustrous, and no doubt the most beautiful fabric material available. It is rarely used because it is quite expensive.

Linen is sometimes used, but though it is tougher than cotton and has all its virtues, it also has all of its flaws, plus a considerably higher price tag.

Wool is a traditional upholstery fabric, long wearing when tightly woven, and attractive. It should be mothproofed and professionally cleaned.

Combinations. Here is another "unfortunately." The statements above about the various fibers are true, but they frequently are not applicable because so many fabrics are combinations of several fibers. When judging a blend the best you can do is work on the basis of the predominant fiber and assume that the characteristics of the blend will resemble those of it.

INFLAMMABILITY

At this writing the laws regulating inflammability are almost nonexistent. The consumer has to depend on his or her own judgment and the conscience of the manufacturer. The industry at large hopes and expects firm laws to be enacted on a national basis sometime early in the 1980s. Until this time, read labels and make a careful decision on this important facet of furnishings.

LEATHER

Natural. Leather is the prince of upholstery materials. Not only is it elegant, it is tough, long lasting and easily cleaned.

Keep it out of direct sunlight, away from radiators and open fires, and good leather upholstery will last 50 years or so. Cleaning is easy; wipe it with a damp cloth. Once in a while, clean the leather with saddle soap and a little water.

All leathers are not equal. The best is 1/16 inch thick or more, supple, and has a shiny surface. A few imperfections here and there do not affect longevity. All leather used for upholstery is split; leather that has a rough surface is suede, the underside of the split, and the less desirable. Leather that feels paper thin when you get a fold between your fingers is also not a good choice.

Synthetic. The best known synthetic leathers are Koroseal and Naugahyde. These and others have many tiny holes that allow air to pass through, making for more comfortable seating. They also have a leatherlike surface texture; they feel supple to the touch and are as thick as good leather. The undesirable imi-

Leather, the finest upholstery material of all, here in a tufted armchair with welted edges.

tation leathers are hard, shiny, thin, and stiff to the touch. They are easily ripped and may become brittle with age.

Purchasing upholstery fabrics. You can purchase furniture already upholstered, in which case you get what you see. Or you can buy the piece in muslin and select the cover fabric yourself. Remember that the style of the piece and the method of upholstering is just about fixed at this point. You cannot easily alter the contours of the arms, and you cannot always opt to have welts or to vary the flounces.

Since the final upholstery material takes most of the wear, and is subjected to all the soiling, this is not a good place to economize. You must select the color and pattern with care. Again we will repeat what we strongly believe; powerful colors and color combinations are for show in books and magazines, not in most homes.

Some furniture buyers insist upon getting a sample swatch of the upholstery fabrics they have ordered, just to preclude mistakes. Naturally, selecting a fabric will cost you more than accepting what is already on the furniture.

DESIGNING OR DECORATING THE LIVING ROOM

An earlier chapter discussed an overall approach to interior decorating or designing. Here, we will make some suggestions for designing your living room.

We start with a number of fixed quantities: the room itself, its size, the number, size and location of windows and doors. The budget is certainly a limiting factor and should be fairly well fixed in your mind before you begin. Almost everything else is up to you. Don't limit yourself to what others may suggest or what you may believe is "in fashion." Follow your own taste and instincts.

Furniture size and shape. Don't select pieces so large that you have little free space in your living room. No matter how large the room may be, there will always be occasions when all your guests will be unable to sit down at once. So just satisfy your everyday seating needs. And remember, no furniture looks good when crowded. If your room is of moderate size, select a three-seat couch or even a love seat in place of a four-seat or larger couch.

Unless your room is small, do not limit yourself to furniture designed to be placed against a wall. Couches, chairs and small tables can be grouped away from walls.

All furniture need not have straight backs. (Obviously, curved-back furniture is designed to be placed away from a wall.)

Everything does not have to match. Years ago it was customary for all the pieces in a living room except tables to be overstuffed and constructed in the same style. This is neither wrong nor right; it need not be a rigid rule. Make your living room reflect the interests and activities of your own household. Remember, you are going to pay for it all, and you and your family, not the casual visitor or relative, are going to live with it.

Styles. A style is a particular, recognizable design that is more or less duplicated in all the pieces that go to make up a set. There are hundreds of styles. They are important to manufac-

Everything doesn't have to match for a well-integrated room. Here the plain color tufted armchair, patterned sofa and checked upholstered chair combine well for an effect of quiet elegance.

turers and salespeople in that they provide a simple means of description. Beyond that they have no importance. No style is "in" and no style is "out." Select style on the basis of what appeals to you; nothing else is of any importance.

Colors. Fabric colors used for upholstery range from black through all the shades of the rainbow to white. Green is the color must of us find easy on the eyes. Orange is the color which makes most of us feel good. Bars and the like are often lit in shades of orange. White shows soil most quickly and black leathers and imitation leathers show soil the least; on fabric dark tan or light brown hides soil best.

Color is deceptive. A swatch of colored cloth does not have anything near the visual impact the same color will have when on an entire sofa chair. No matter how attractive the color may be in a swatch, a "strong" color will drive you bonkers if you cover the furniture with it.

It is our opinion that the brightest color in a living room should be the pictures on the wall and the people in the room. The rest of the room should be a muted background. We there fore recommend muted colors, quiet colors; colors that do not call attention to themselves. They do not have to be neutral grays or gray browns. They can be any hue as long as they do not overpower the viewer.

You cannot place a bright grass-green next to a tomato red and expect visual harmony, but when the colors are soft and grayed-down, they will look well side by side.

Patterns. There are three basic fabric patterns used for upholstery: solid (no pattern), stripes, and figures.

You may think a solid color will be visually dull. Not so. When the upholstery fabric is a solid color, the upholstery does not "fight" the shape of the furniture. A single color gives rise to a more definite feeling: This is a brown chair, this is a blue. A single color is like a single pure musical note. It is never cacophonous. Another plus for the solid color is that it is easier to work with.

A patterned fabric may seem to be one color from a distance and another close up. A greater handicap is that patterns break up the visual image so that it is difficult to perceive the actual outline of the furniture. When the pattern is really strong and bright, one sees it upon entering the room and not the furniture. Whatever beauty there may be in the shape of the furniture is lost.

Patterns are fine when they are muted, subdued, and blend readily into the overall fabric. When they dominate the room they become ugly and obtrusive.

Stripes are a special form of pattern. They are visually very powerful. Not everyone finds them attractive. They belong only on very stiff, formal, and straight furniture: couches with straight backs, straight-sided chairs, etc. Take the time to evaluate fully the visual effect of a striped piece of furniture in your home before you buy it.

Patterned, pictorial upholstery against a large, solid-finish chest. The result has an Oriental feeling, to which the rug contributes.

7

Bedroom Furniture

Bedroom furniture closely resembles kitchen and dining room furniture in materials and construction. The only bedroom furniture that is upholstered is really living room furniture brought into the bedroom. Some people will fill out a large bedroom with a chaise longue, others prefer to have a small table and two small chairs for a cozy, intimate breakfast. With the exception of these and the bed itself, bedroom furniture consists of cabinets and chests constructed along the same mechanical lines as similar pieces in other parts of the house. Most of the criteria suggested for selecting kitchen and dining room furniture, therefore, are applicable to bedroom furniture.

DESIGNING THE BEDROOM

The rules for designing or decorating a bedroom differ from the ones to follow for other rooms in your home.

Color. Most of us can tolerate, or will even prefer, fairly strong although not fully saturated, color in our bedrooms. (Fully saturated color is color as strong as is available.)

Color can be used on walls, in curtains, bedspreads, and rugs. If the rug or curtain is relatively small, the color can be fairly strong. But you should hold to two rules as a guide.

A single color is best of all. Two colors can be pleasing, but when you go beyond two the problems of tone and compassionate blending become very difficult, especially as the strength of the colors increases.

The use of a single color for a bedroom may appear to be limiting, but it is not so by any means. (The great Gainsborough did his famous *Blue Boy* painting in tones of blue alone.) If you choose blue, for example, your walls can be basically a white to which some cerulean blue has been added. The rug can be a darker shade and the curtains can be a lighter shade of the same blue. The furniture could also be blue or a neutral gray. It will all blend in beautifully. But unless you have experience you will not know whether another color, or even a different blue, will blend in well until you try it.

To test a color, without actually buying the piece, try a large piece of cardboard painted that color where the furniture will be.

Clutter. There is less traffic in the bedroom, so less space is required between pieces of furniture. Remember, though, that a bedroom is where you will be moving around in the dark, so don't clutter it with unnecessary furniture. The fewer the pieces in a room, the easier it is to keep tidy and clean.

Positioning. Two factors are important to remember. A bed placed near an inner wall will be warmer than one placed near an exterior wall. A bed placed between two opposing win-

Bedrooms need clear space around the furniture, especially if they are to include lounging facilities, as in this spacious room with its comfortable armchair and hassock.

A platform bed in an alcove. The mattresses and springs are set on a wooden platform. Such an arrangement is ideal for a dual-purpose room in a small apartment, especially when the bed can be closed off with folding doors, as in this photograph.

dows or between a door and a window will derive the benefit of whatever breeze is stirring during the summer.

If your neighborhood is noisy, place the head of the bed *out* of line with the windows. Sound enters through an open or closed window in a more or less straight line, the way light does. A carpet under the bed will somewhat insulate it from sounds from below. A bed placed close to any wall will pick up more internal sounds than a bed placed a distance away.

DRESSERS, BUREAUS, CHIFFONIERS, ETC.

A dresser is a chest of drawers with a vertical mirror on top. A dressing table is a chest of small, parallel drawers separated by a space for knees and a mirror on top; sometimes with two small mirrors on hinges at either side of a larger central one. Bureaus are chests of drawers, on legs of varying lengths and tops about as high as a dining room table—29 inches. A chiffonier is a tall, comparatively narrow chest of drawers topped by a small vertical mirror. The top of the chest portion of the chiffonier is usually 4 feet above the floor or even higher.

Painted furniture is practical in a bedroom, where the surfaces do not require constant wiping, as in a kitchen or dining room. This room, with its built-in furniture, has a bright, modern look.

Although the shapes are different, the materials and method of construction are alike, and quite similar if not identical to those used in sideboards, servers, and the like. Thus the criteria you use in selecting these pieces are similar to those that govern the selection of dining room chests, with one exception.

Finish. Bedroom furniture may be finished in any of the ways other wooden furniture is. But whereas we warned you away from painted finishes for other rooms, there is no objection to painted bedroom furniture. A chest of drawers in a bedroom will not see one tenth the use of a dining room table, and hardly any of the wear and tear to which a kitchen table is subjected. Thus a painted finish will wear well on bedroom furniture.

BEDS

Size. The accepted rule is that a mattress be at least 6 inches longer than the height of the tallest sleeper. The width depends on you. You have a choice of double bed, queen size, or king size, or a single or twin bed for one sleeper. There are some special sizes as well (see "mattress sizes," page 112.)

Costs. Whether two singles cost more or less than a double will depend on the beds you select and the store from which you make your purchase. What you may not realize is that the linens, blankets, pillows, covers and mattresses for the king, queen, prince, and other extra-large beds do not cost just a few pennies more; they cost about 50% more than "Full regular."

Floor space. Walk-about space in the bedroom should not be lightly dismissed. One does not do much walking in a bedroom, but much of it is eyes-shut walking. If your bed is so large that there is less than 2 feet around it, there are going to be a lot of bruised shins. If it is so large it has to be flush against an outside wall, that wall may be cold in winter and hot in summer. If there is noise on the other side of the wall, it will seem magnified if the bed touches the wall.

Bed types or designs.

Wood frame bed. This consists of a headboard, a footboard, and two side rails, which hook into the head and footboards to form a rectangle. Two strips of wood are fastened to the inside surfaces of the side rails. Then wooden slats are placed across the bed frame, their ends resting on the wooden inner strips of the side rails. The springs and mattress lay on the slats. If you jump on this type of bed the slats may move sideways and the springs fall. It is easily, if bothersomely, replaced.

The basic wood frame design can be varied a hundred different ways. Head and footboards can be large, small, straight-sided, carved, clear-finished, or painted and decorated with pictures. They can be of one-piece construction or can have corner posts. If the corner posts are very long and tall, the bed becomes a four-poster. If the tops of the posts are connected by boards, you have a canopy bed.

Any bed made with more than a modicum of care should be strong enough for its task. But some have not been this

A traditional wooden four-poster bed in early American style.

carefully made. Inspect the joints between the cleats and side rails. The better beds have wood screws here, not nails and glue. Inspect the "hook" joint between the side rails and the head and footboards. Have the salesman take the joint apart by lifting the side rail. Check to see how firmly the metal hook is fastened in place. See that there are no cracks in the ends of the side rail, nor in the corners of the head and footboards.

Since the bed itself is subjected to very little wear over the years, almost any finish can be used. Beds can be painted, veneered, or varnished.

If there are corner posts, inspect the joints between the posts and the head and footboards. If the boards are veneered, the front of the headboard and both sides of the footboard should be also veneered. In some instances the side rails will be veneered as well. (Their top edges may or may not be.) None of this matters if you plan to cover this part of the bed with a spread.

If the bed is painted, the back of the headboard should also be painted, just as both sides of the footboard should be painted.

It is best that the bed be mounted on casters and that the casters be large, preferably with ball rollers and a stop to lock them in place. They make cleaning beneath the bed that much easier. Larger casters roll, but small casters tend to dig into the floor or carpet.

If you want a firmer support than that provided by a spring, replace it with plywood. Use two sheets of low-grade (rough surface) 3/8-inch plywood. Don't trouble to cut them lengthwise. Just let them overlap. Fasten one to the other with a few wood screws. Lay your mattress on top of the wood.

Metal frame beds. Like the wood frame bed, there is a headboard and a footboard, but they are made of metal. The metal may be in the form of painted, chrome-plated or brass-plated pipe, or of sheet metal made to resemble a wooden headboard. The side rails are angle irons and terminate in wedges that fit into slots in the head and footboard. To separate the side rails from the head and footboard, tap the undersides of the rail ends with a hammer. At the same time, hold on to the head or footboard. It will topple when the rail comes loose.

This type of bed was very popular not too many years ago because it was very inexpensive and durable. The old beds had very strong side rails. The new ones do not. Push down on the center of a side rail. Naturally, the rail will give under your weight, but if it gives too easily and you could put a permanent bend in it if you half tried, it is too thin. It will hold the spring, mattress, and sleepers without a problem, but if someone accidentally sits down on the side rail or if kids jump on the bed, it will be damaged.

The springs made for these old metal beds have short hooks at their sides. These hooks hold the spring in place and prevent it from sliding sideways off the frame. If you place any other type of spring on top, use galvanized wire to fasten it in place.

Modern steel frames. These are angle-iron frames mounted on short metal legs which are in turn supported by casters. Since the angle iron that forms the frame is narrow, any spring an inch or two too small will fall through, and oversized springs simply will not fit. Purchase spring and bed together and try them together or measure the width *very, very* carefully.

Some modern steel frames are drilled to accept bolts that may be used to fasten head and footboards. Naturally the holes in the frame must line up with the holes in the side boards. If they do not or there are no holes in frame or boards you must either forgo the head and footboards, drill holes, or lean the headboard up against a wall and back the bed end against it.

This type of bed is very popular, and is stocked in greater quantity than any other kind. They are inexpensive, space efficient, and strong.

When inspecting a bed of this type first make certain it will fit your spring, then check to see that all the legs are firm, all the rivets in place and tight, and the casters free to roll and turn.

Platform beds. These are simply platforms on which the spring and mattress rest. The common design consists of a single sheet or joined sheets of plywood to form a deck. The deck rests on a box-shaped support. Most often the deck overhangs the support by 6 or more inches. Platform beds are made with and without headboards. When it is backed up against a wall there is no need for a headboard, which only serves to keep the pillows in place. If desired, any suitable independent headboard can be positioned between the bed end and the wall.

Some platform beds are sold with accompanying headboards that incorporate amenities such as a night light, a radio, drawers, shelves, and other conveniences.

Platform beds may be finished any way wood is finished. Since the finish will not be subjected to much wear, one is as good as another. And since the load on the deck and support is very light, the strength of the wood and the joints is not a consideration. Just make certain the joints are tight, the finish is even, and the size correct. (Remember, you do not want wood projecting beyond the edge of your mattress.)

Springs are not usually used on platform beds. The mattress lies directly on the platform itself.

Box spring beds. Box springs, which are described more fully a bit later on, are constructed on a wooden frame. To convert the box spring to a bed, four legs are fastened to the underside of the spring with large, central screws. When the box frame is of thick hardwood, and the legs are equally strong and well fastened, you have a reasonably permanent bed. But since these beds are usually made to sell at a low price, the wood frame is of soft pine. When the bed is tilted during cleaning or when children jump on it the legs can rip loose and the bed will fall.

You can easily judge the quality of these beds by lifting them. The weak ones are very light in weight. Look at the underside. If it is made of pine, you can tell by its pale yellow color.

If you do buy this bed and the legs do get knocked off, remove them and let the box spring rest on the floor. You still have a useful bed.

Or you can buy an adjustable metal frame with castered legs in which to set the box spring and mattress.

Convertible beds. The best, to our way of thinking, is the simplest—the trundle bed. One half serves as a settee during the day. The second and smaller half is on rollers beneath the first. Simply pull it out from under to have two single beds. There are no springs, joints or moving parts to get stuck, wear out, or

A more common answer to the dual-purpose room—the "sleep sofa" that converts to a bed.

break. But you do have to move the second mattress from atop the settee and make the bed up each time you use it.

If you select a folding bed, try it several times to make certain it works smoothly. See that nothing has to be forced to fit and that it can be closed as easily as it can be opened. See too that its design is such that you cannot catch your fingers and hands, and that it is not so complicated that it is going to go out of whack very quickly.

Inspect the upholstered portion of the folding bed just as you would upholstered or overstuffed furniture. Follow the same criteria in making your decision.

Select a bed that does not require special size sheets and blankets or a special mattress. You do not want to be in the position of discarding a folding bed in good condition when the mattress is worn because you cannot find a new one that fits.

One more point. Check both the open and closed space requirements of the bed you are considering before buying it. Their open lengths vary with the design. Some need several more feet of space when they are open than others.

FOUNDATIONS (SPRINGS)

Today bed springs that support mattresses are often called foundations; by any name, they are still springs.

Flat springs. A number of thin, flat strips of steel are criss-crossed and fastened to a metal frame by small coil springs. The result is a flat surface that will give beneath the weight of a body much like a hammock. The strips of metal do not stretch with use, but the coil springs do, so in time the flat metal spring develops a permanent sag near the center. The springs cannot be tightened, but they can be replaced.

Flat springs do not provide maximum comfort and they do not last forever. However, flat springs will last considerably longer than coil springs.

Coil springs. Each coil is made of spring steel wire and may be 3 to 5 inches across and up to about 12 inches high when free.

The coils are positioned side by side between two large frames of thick wire. The springs are compressed and fastened to each other and to the frames with wire or thin flat bands of metal. The end result is a single "spring" anywhere from 6 to 9 inches high that will support a mattress.

The advantage of the coil arrangement is that each spring is free to some degree to act individually. They conform to the shape of the body. That is why many people find this type of foundation or bed spring most comfortable of all.

There was a time when it was possible to purchase a coil spring foundation without any covering at all. While there was a savings in doing this the springs collected dust and pressed directly on the underside of the mattress and so increased its rate of wear.

Today, coil spring foundations are covered with a layer of padding, and over that, tightly fitted ticking. The better coil spring foundations have vent holes on their sides and strong handles. Foundations should be turned every six months or so, alternating a side-to-side with an end-to-end turn. This extends their life considerably.

The most commonly used padding is cotton, followed by one of the plastic foams and then by sisal, a strong vegetable fiber. The life of the padding will depend upon its thickness as well as on the material. Since the spring assembly is sealed, all you can do is press down on the foundation to see that it indeed has a pad on both sides.

Ticking made of synthetic fiber is better here than the cotton ticking so often used in the past. When the two are of equal thickness, the synthetic fiber outlasts the natural several times over. In addition, the synthetics are not as easily ignited as cotton. The one major caution here is against vinyl. It is not easily ignited but produces toxic fumes when it burns. In any case, read the label to determine the foundation contents, and try to get a fold of the ticking between your fingers to help you judge its thickness. Also examine the workmanship: the stitching, the welts, how even the fabric is. Pay no attention to the colors. You don't see them when you are asleep.

Box springs. A box spring foundation is constructed much like a standard coil spring foundation. In addition to the lower wire frame or in place of it there is a wood frame and cross members of either steel or wood. When they fit, these foundations can be used in place of standard coil spring foundations. But that is not the reason for their design.

Box springs are made to eliminate the bed frame. Thus you will find short legs screwed to the underside corners of box springs. With a mattress on top, you have a complete bed, one without head and footboards.

To evaluate a box spring, lift it. The heavier the better. Look for hardwood and steel bottom supports. Read the label. Look for a muslin dustcover over its bottom. Avoid box springs with excelsior stuffing or very thin ticking. They won't last a year.

MATTRESSES

MATTRESS SIZES*

(Obviously, you will need springs and a frame of consonant size.)

NAME	WIDTH (INCHES)	LENGTH (INCHES)
Child's bed	30-34	75
Twin regular	39	75
Twin king (extra long)	39	80-84
Full regular	54	75
Full king (extra long)	54	80-84
Queen regular	60	75
Queen king (extra long)	60	80-84
King regular	76	75
King king (extra long)	76	80-84
Eastern king	78	80
California king	72	84

*If you find yourself unable to sleep, count mattress sizes instead of sheep.

Innerspring mattresses. There are two types of innerspring mattresses: open coil and pocketed coil.

The open coil innerspring mattress is constructed like the coil spring foundation described previously, but the springs are made of thinner, more flexible wire, and considerably more padding is used on top of the spring.

Generally the innerspring mattress and its foundation are manufactured by the same company. They are made in pairs; exactly the same overall size and thickness and usually covered with ticking of the same pattern.

The pocketed coil innerspring mattresses differ in that each coil is enclosed in a cloth pocket and all the pockets are joined to one another. Except for the cloth, the springs are in no way joined to one another. The manufacturers claim that this is a mattress that most nearly conforms to the sleeper's body and so provides a more comfortable, more restful sleep.

Open coil mattresses have some 180 to 300 coils each. Pocketed coil mattresses may have as many as 800 coils per mattress and some have as many as 1,000 individual steel coils in individual cloth pockets.

Supposedly, the more coils in either type of mattress the more comfortable that mattress is, but this is strictly a question of personal preference.

Padding and ticking. The top surfaces of both types of innerspring mattress are covered with padding enclosed in ticking. Many materials can be used for the padding. On the better mattresses, the padding consists of an inner layer, usually called the insulation, and an outer layer, usually called the cushioning.

Mattress insulation may be of cotton, hog hair, or sisal. Cushioning may consist of cotton, latex (rubber), urethane foam, or horse or hog hair dipped in rubber. Which is best? Again, unfortunately, this cannot be answered helpfully. Not only do we have to consider the individual material, we have to know its grade and we have to consider its thickness. A generous thickness of a low-grade padding can be more desirable than a thin layer of a top-grade padding.

The better (and wiser) mattress manufacturers supply stores with see-in samples of their products. Thus you can inspect the innards, see how thick the padding is and sometimes the type of construction. If you also read the label, which by law must be attached to each mattress, you can learn a little more about what you are considering.

The thicker the padding the better. The two-layer padding arrangement is better, assuming that the total padding thickness of both pads is thicker than the single pad or nearly equal to it. Virgin material is always far better than processed or reprocessed material. We would list rubberized horse or hog hair as best for the insulation, and choose ½ inch of hair in place of 1 inch of cotton. However, horse or hog hair is very scarce. Most manufacturers use cotton for their insulation.

For the cushioning we would choose urethane foam over latex or an equal or even slightly thicker pad of latex and urethane over a cotton layer that is as much as one third thicker.

If the manufacturer of the mattress has not seen fit to provide you with an interior view of his product, all you can do is lift the mattress, and then press down on it. Lifting will give you an indication of its relative weight. Generally, but not always, the heavier mattress is the better choice. Pressing down will give you a very rough evaluation of the springs and padding. If you can feel the springs, the padding is very thin. You also might lie down on the mattress and bounce around a little.

Many people choose cotton for mattress covers, believing correctly that it is cooler and more comfortable than any synthetic. Cotton does, however, have a lower ignition temperature. All the criteria mentioned in regard to foundation covers also hold for evaluating mattress covers or ticking.

Foam mattresses. In our opinion the best is made of urethane without core holes or any other spaces that reduce its weight and life expectancy. The slab of foam should be wrapped in several layers of dacron before being sewn into its bag. The denser and thicker the urethane the longer it will retain its shape. Again, when choosing between two urethane foam mattresses, weight is an important factor.

Stuffed mattresses. This is the least expensive type of mattress available today, but it is hard to come by. It consists of a flat cloth bag stuffed with any one of a number of soft materials. The best stuffing is horsehair dipped in rubber.

Firmness. Innerspring mattresses are made in three or four degrees of firmness. Unfortunately one manufacturer's designation has little relation to another's. One company's "firm" may be another's "ultra-firm." The only trustworthy way to compare is to lie down on each mattress.

Backaches. The best support for a weak and painful back is a stuffed mattress supported by a board—any kind of board. So don't waste your money on "orthopedic" mattresses. They never provide as firm a support as a stuffed mattress on a board. Once you become accustomed to this type of bed, you will find any other uncomfortably soft.

8

Wicker and Rattan

DEFINITIONS

Wicker is the general term for furniture material woven from any plant fibers. The term includes such materials as sea grass, rush, reed, splint, parts of leaves, grass, willow and other thin-branched, flexible trees and bushes, cane, bamboo, and rattan. But rattan is never classified as a wicker; it is always designated rattan.

Willow. The surface is smooth and firm with a few tiny imperfections. Willow takes paint and varnish well, is strong and like all wood is long lasting if not permitted to remain wet. An occasional hosing will do it no harm, but if left on grass or bare earth it will show rot in one season. Most willows used are about 3/8 inch thick or less. Better willow furniture is tightly woven. Care is taken that no ends show and there are no breaks near the bends. The end of a willow twig is solid wood.

Sea grass. A ropelike fiber made by twisting types of dry seaweed. It comes in a number of gauges or thicknesses. It is shiny and hard. The strand itself is not solid but shows the twisted fibers. Diameter normally varies a little along the length of the woven grass. Its natural color is a greenish brown, but the material is usually stained. Open an end and you can see the strands of grass.

Sea grass is used for weaving seat backs and bottoms. It makes a coarse, hard, shiny surface that is long lasting, again if not permitted to stay wet. Generally it is not varnished or similarly finished.

Replacing a sea grass seat or back is not difficult and can be accomplished by a beginner in several hours with material purchased from a craft supply shop.

Rush. "Rush" is an artificial fiber made by twisting Kraft paper upon itself or upon a central wire core. It is usually much thinner than sea grass and much smoother but it retains the folded edges of the paper. Rush is woven into seats and backs of furniture. While the result is as pleasing and smooth as sea grass, rush cannot withstand water *at all*. If thoroughly soaked, it may come apart.

Usually, rush is coated with varnish or paint before or after it is woven. Not being as hard as the other wickers, rush weavings do not last nearly as long.

If rush has to be replaced in a chair seat or back, it is best to use another material, such as cane or sea grass.

In addition to being used for backs and seats, rush is often machine woven and placed on top of a furniture frame, much the way a seat cover is fabricated and placed upon a seat. This is the inexpensive way of making wicker furniture. The appearance is fair to good and so long as the furniture doesn't get soaked, it will last many years.

Properly designed wicker furniture can come in from the porch and out of the playroom to look surprisingly good in a somewhat more formal setting.

A "summer" room, with wicker everywhere. Different weaves and widths keep the effect from seeming either monotonous or overpowering.

Very often when the rush becomes shabby it is painted. This may help for a little while and may be the only practical alternative to discarding the piece, but excessive paint makes the rush brittle. It tends to crack after being painted; to minimize this cracking, use a very light coat of paint.

You can easily recognize paper rush by taking an end apart.

Reed. Reed is the generic term for any tall, slender grass, especially those that grow in wet and swampy areas. Egyptian papyrus is a reed, and so is the American cottontail. Reeds are used for basketry and furniture. But "reed" as used by American craftsmen and in this book is not a genuine reed but the core of rattan (which is described in more detail a bit later on).

The core is split into one of a number of shapes—either round, oval, or flat—and into pieces with diameters of from 1/16 inch to several inches. It is moderately flexible when dry, very flexible after being soaked. Upon drying it will hold, more or less, to the same shape it was in when soaked.

Reed is easily recognized. Its ends always show a number of evenly spaced black dots, which are actually fine holes or pores. Its natural color is a pale tan. The surface has many fine parallel ridges running the length of the reed, which may be as long as 20 feet. Reed takes stain well and can be varnished and painted.

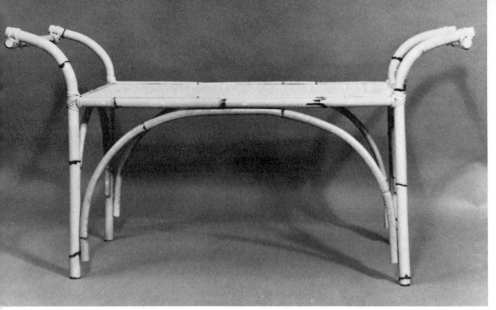

A bench of rattan.

Paint applied too heavily, however, or in too many successive coats tends to produce dry rot and weaken the reed.

Reed is used in furniture to form arms and sides and backs of chairs and couches. It is also used as flat material—a splint—for backs and seats. Almost always the woven reed will be supported on a wooden frame. Reed furniture is light in weight, long lasting if it is not permitted to stand on earth or remain wet too long. It is flexible and often squeaks when someone moves on it.

Reed furniture quality can be estimated by the density of the weave and the neatness of the exposed ends of the piece. For example, an inexpensively made piece will have a number of reed ends showing at the end of the arm and tied into a bundle with another piece of reed. On a better made piece, the reed ends will be folded back and rewoven into the whole so that no ends are showing.

Reed is highly absorbent and should always be given at least a light coat of varnish. Otherwise it will be permanently soiled. Hose reed furniture to clean it. Water will not harm it.

Splint. Originally splint was made by splitting a very thin strip from the edge of a board. Today, this method is still used, but in addition reed is split into splint.

Splint is about 1/64 inch thick and about ¾ inch wide. The lengths run to 6 or 8 feet. In furniture construction, splint is used almost exclusively for weaving seat bottoms and backs.

Woven splint is durable and comfortable. The weave itself is open and usually of a simple pattern. Wood splint is preferred to reed splint, but wood splint is much more costly and a little more difficult to weave. Both should be given at least one sealing coat of varnish. Both can be cleaned with water. Splint is generally limited to Shaker style and similar "rustic" furniture.

Splint is moderately easy to weave and can be used, if desired, to replace other seating material that may be damaged.

Cane. The core of rattan is "reed," the skin or surface of the rattan just above the reed is cane. It is removed from the rattan pole in long, narrow strips. One side of the strip is a pale yellow and very hard. The underside looks like reed.

Cane is very strong and long lasting. When soaked, it is fairly flexible, and in this condition it is used to weave chair seats and back by hand. The process is slow, difficult and time consuming. Little hand weaving is done today. Instead, the cane is machine woven into a tough, coarse kind of cloth and the cloth forms the seat or back of the chair or other piece.

As for wearing and appearance, there is no difference between the two, except for purists. However, there is a tremendous difference when it comes to repair. A machine-woven cane seat can be replaced in less than a hour. A hand-woven seat may take all day.

You can recognize hand-woven cane furniture by the holes that ring the edges of the cane. To be certain, look at the underside of the piece. In some cases, a parallel strip of cane is locked beneath the ends of the cane weaving. This strip is parallel to the edges of the weaving and is almost exactly in the same place you'd find a spline.

A machine-woven cane seat, back, tabletop, etc., is woven so that the edges terminate beneath a spline. This is a wedge-shaped length of cane that has been forced into a groove running along the edges of the weave. The wedge or spline locks the edges of the machine-woven cane in place. To replace this cane, you need but remove the spline, position the new cane and then drive a new spline back in the groove. (See page 209-211.)

Normally, cane is never varnished or painted. Its surface is naturally coated with silicon. Cane must be moistened regularly if it is not to dry out and break. Some authorities say moisten the cane once a month; others say once in six months is plenty. To moisten cane, hose it. If that is not practical, turn the piece over and press a wet sponge to the underside. Hold the sponge in place a minute or two. That will do it.

Properly cared for, cane will last a century or more. Soiled cane can be washed with soap and water.

Cane is also used to wrap or bind rattan furniture joints. This cane too, must be kept moist. The same methods suggested for seat cane may be used.

RATTAN

Rattan is the generic name for a number of climbing palm trees native to the jungles of the Far East.

At this writing there are more than 150 known species that are harvested and used. They are generally designated by the regions from which they come: Tahiti, Pakkie, Kooboo, Oemoeloe, and Loontie. One is as good as another in finished furniture.

Rattan is also classified by diameter and appearance. The thicker poles are more difficult to work with, but generally look better in the completed furniture. They also cost more. "Cleaner" rattan with fewer burn marks and other imperfections is also considered more desirable by many people.

Skinned rattan furniture. Rattan that has had the surface removed as cane is often used for the undersides of furniture or otherwise hidden by a continuous wrapping of cane, as it is rough in texture. If the roughness is removed, we have a thick or fat reed up to 2 inches in diameter. Many modern furniture makers use this skinned rattan for furniture making. It is bent more easily and evenly than regular rattan. Its surface is smooth and clean.

From the purchaser's point of view it has two drawbacks. It looks more like plastic pipe than rattan. Some buyers prefer this appearance. Also, the tough, silicon coating of the rattan has been removed and replaced by a layer of varnish. When the varnish wears through, the furniture owner must replace it before the soft, porous reed is stained. But this is easily done by sanding the bare spot and spraying it with varnish.

Reed core. When the yellow outer surface of the rattan is removed the remainder is a solid reed. It can be used as is or may be split into different shapes and thicknesses.

HOW RATTAN FURNITURE IS MADE

Rattan made by hand overseas is bent by first wetting the pole with water and then holding it over a torch flame. The result usually shows a little burn mark, which adds to its charm. Factory-made rattan is bent in a steam box, and rarely shows burn marks. The pieces of foreign-made rattan are usually nailed together, with cane used to bind or wrap the joint and hide the nail head. Nailed joints come apart when the piece of furniture is subjected to any stress. Most of the better rattan made here is joined with wood screws. The best has mortise and tenon joints, *plus* screws *and* glue.

EVALUATING RATTAN FURNITURE

Design is a matter of taste. These are the other features that make one piece of rattan furniture better than another:

Thicker frame members are not only stronger, but take and hold screws and joints more securely.

Neat cane wrappings.

Closely fitting pieces with little or no space between the ends of the rattan and the sides of other pieces.

Mortise and tenon joints with screws or screwed joints alone rather than nailed joints.

Varnish where the natural silicon came off near a bend (this always happens when rattan is sharply bent).

A frame that doesn't give much when you sit or lean on it; that feels stiff and sturdy.

Ends that have been sanded a little so there are no sharp edges.

A frame in which all the pieces are securely fastened.

BAMBOO

Bamboo is hard, flexible, and hollow at its center with cross plugs at the joints. It is often used for inexpensive furniture and painted irregularly to imitate the markings and burns natural to rattan. Bamboo is also pale yellow and has no natural markings. There is a circumferential ridge at the joints. Rattan has no joints and the markings at the leaf points are rough and sometimes dark edged.

Bamboo cannot be bent like rattan, therefore bamboo furniture is always made of straight pieces. While bamboo is flexible and springy like rattan and is as tough and time resistant, bamboo furniture joints are far less strong than good rattan joints.

The root of the bamboo plant looks much like human knuckle bones. You will often see these roots used for small objects like picture frames.

9

Outdoor Furniture

WOOD FURNITURE

Redwood. The best wood for outdoor furniture. It is literally red throughout and impervious to rot and insects. It will last a long, long time, even if left directly on earth and exposed to wind, rain, sun, and snow. The wood, however, is comparatively weak so the pieces should be at least 1½ inches thick.

Redwood is also used in combination with various metals. In such cases the wood is usually about ¾ inch thick and supported by metal brackets and similar assemblies. It is difficult therefore to judge the strength and weather resistance of such pieces. We know the wood will not deteriorate, but how fast will the metal go, and will it rust and discolor the wood? The heavier piece of furniture with the thicker pieces of metal and wood will probably stand up to wear better. Chances are the edges of the metal and the nuts and bolts will rust, because the edges of the metal are usually not plated and the bolts are usually of iron. (Plating the edges involves considerably extra labor and cost. If the edges are plated, you will see no color difference between the surface and the edge, and the edge will not have a very sharp, almost knifelike corner.)

Poplar and fir. Poplar is a very pale, whitish wood, lighter in weight and weaker by far than fir. Fir is a bit on the yellow side with prominent, resin-filled grain. Neither wood is rot resistant. Both are used interchangeably in lower-priced outdoor furniture. Both are stained to imitate redwood. To check, cut a sliver from the undersurface of these woods; you will see the original color.

Both woods will last in outdoor use a long time if you make certain they do not rest directly on soil, and you take them indoors in the winter.

Repairs. All-wood outdoor furniture usually suffers from weak joints, especially lower-priced pieces. Instead of wood screws, the pieces are often joined by machine-driven staples. When the pieces come loose, join them again with wood screws.

IRON

Cast iron. This is very heavy and highly ornamental; the pieces are gracefully curved with intricate decorative patterns. Cast iron is probably the most expensive of all outdoor furniture. To a degree it is indestructible. It can withstand rain, insects, and rot. However, cast iron is brittle. A heavy rock, thrown in play, can crack it. And I would not leave cast iron uncovered in frosty weather. Iron is not damaged by frost, but castings often contain tiny voids that can hold water. When the water freezes, it expands and can crack the iron.

In winter, cover cast iron furniture with a sheet of plastic. The enclosed water will dry out and will not be replaced.

When the paint wears off, cast iron furniture can simply be repainted. If the iron rusts, remove the rust with a steel wire brush. There is no need to prime the iron with red lead paint; it won't do much to prevent rusting.

Wrought iron. Actually mild steel, this furniture is made by bending and welding bars and rods of various dimensions.

The more desirable wrought iron furniture is made of heavy, thick pieces of steel. All the weld joints have been ground smooth; there are no openings, or voids, in the joints. If the furniture is ornamented, the ornaments are made of steel that has been hand wrought on a forge. Each turn and curlicue is a bit different from its neighbors.

The less desirable wrought iron furniture is made from thinner stock, weighs less, is often joined by nuts and bolts and the ornaments, if any, are of thin pieces of pressed steel.

The very best wrought iron furniture is solidly plated with copper. This cuts rusting to a minimum. All you need do with it is paint it once in a while.

All wrought iron furniture can be left out in any weather. Nothing short of a hurricane can harm it.

ALUMINUM

The better aluminum furniture is made by welding thick tubes of aluminum together to form a frame. Support is provided by bands of solid plastic. You can easily recognize welded-tube furniture by the absence of joints and nuts and bolts or rivets. Again, if you are trying to decide between two makes, the heavier is the stronger. But before you accept delivery, examine all the welds. They should be smooth and without voids.

The less desirable and far less expensive aluminum outdoor furniture is made of thin tubes of aluminum. You will recognize this type by its light weight, the presence of rivets—which always rust—and various brackets to hold some of the parts together.

Usually, solid plastic bands are not used to provide body support. Instead a woven web of plastic is used. This will hardly

Quality aluminum and plastic outdoor furniture is light, weather resistant and attractive.

last two seasons if exposed to the weather. The aluminum itself is not affected, but eventually the rivets will rust completely through. Again, overall weight is a good indication of comparative quality, and solid plastic bands or tubes of plastic are much preferable to the woven bands.

But, if you need to fold and carry this type of furniture often and you do not want to spend any more money than need be, there is nothing wrong with thin-tube outdoor furniture.

PLASTIC PIPE

This is not as yet on the market, but we expect it to be shortly. It is light in weight, and resists weather, rot, and insects. Support surfaces are provided either by the pipe itself under a cushion, or by strips of solid or woven plastic.

Weight is not a measure of its quality, but pipe diameter is; the thicker the pipe the stronger the furniture. When you buy, make certain the furniture is guaranteed against sagging in midsummer heat. This is a common fault of plastic pipe.

CUSHIONS

So far as we know, no outdoor cushion is perfectly waterproof. They all will absorb some water if left in a heavy rain. The only answer is to dash out there and bring them in or cover them with a sheet of plastic.

If you permit any of these water resistant cushions to remain in the rain, they will absorb water and rot or mildew.

10

Rugs and Carpets

First, let us clear up any confusion between rugs and carpets. A rug is smaller than the floor on which it lies and is not fastened down. A carpet generally occupies the entire floor, from wall to wall, and is fastened in place.

There are throw rugs, area rugs, room-size rugs, and just plain rugs. All these designations refer to size, but there is really no numerical demarcation. A rug can be cut from a piece of carpet. As long as it is not fastened down, it is a rug.

BASIC DECISIONS

Benefits versus drawbacks. Carpets and rugs add color and beauty to a room. They provide softness underfoot. They soften and mute sounds originating within the room and block some of the sound coming from below. When the carpet is above an unheated area it adds a little warmth to the room.

Carpets require much more care, attention and cleaning than do bare floors. They introduce fine dust into the air unless they are vacuumed frequently.

Carpets versus rugs. Carpets are not investments in the sense that rugs and furniture are. Carpeting can last for many years, but it will not last for generations the way a good, well-cared-for rug does.

You cannot send a carpet out to be cleaned, and in-place cleaning never does nearly as good a job. You can turn a rug so that it is bleached evenly by sunlight coming through a window.

You can't of course do this with carpeting. You can also move and shift a rug so that wear is even; you cannot do this with a carpet.

You can easily move rugs to a new home. But in most instances it does not pay to remove an even slightly used carpet and put it down elsewhere. There is the cost (or your labor) of removing and relaying the carpet. Consider, too, the almost certain chance of waste resulting from the different shape of the new floor, and of purchasing new carpeting to cover areas that cannot be covered by the old, not to mention the problem of matching it.

On the other hand, if your floor is in bad shape, you can cover it with a carpet. If you lay down a rug, you have to refinish the floor, or at least part of it.

There is labor involved in keeping a floor bright and shiny. You have to wax it once in a while. A rug may slip underfoot; a carpet will not.

Wall-to-wall carpeting will also enhance the value and saleability of your home. It is customary to include carpeting in the price of a home, but not rugs.

Still another point to consider when choosing between carpeting and rugs is resale. You will be lucky to recover 10% of your original cost when you remove and resell carpeting. Rugs are easily sold and the return will always be proportionally much higher and possibly even profitable.

What color? If you have the furniture on hand and wish to select a rug or carpet color to enhance it, your safest approach is to buy a few sheets of showcard cardboard in or near the color you are considering. Place the cardboard on the floor. Make your decision after seeing it both during daylight hours and in the evening when the room is artificially illuminated. The cardboard only costs a few dollars. (If you have a bath mat of the desired color you can also use it to help you decide.)

Patterns. Both rugs and carpeting can be had in patterns. Rugs have borders, patterned carpets do not. Patterned carpets are more costly than solid colors because there is always waste when carpet sections have to be matched so as not to break the pattern. In addition, most people find patterns from wall to wall overpowering. You can, of course, combine patterned carpeting with solid color carpeting so as to produce borders and the like. Naturally the labor and cost of laying the carpet will then be increased.

What rug size? You are selecting a rug to go on the living-room floor between facing pieces of furniture. There will be a small table on the rug. A rug smaller than the table would look strange. A rug just as large as the table means the table legs will rest on the rug edges. A rug just a little larger than the table will look like a doily.

You want the rug to be larger than the central table by at least a foot on each side. On the other hand you do not want the rug to terminate a few inches from the other furniture. There should be at least one foot of open space between the furniture legs and the edges of the rug, or else the rug should run all the way under the furniture.

Position your furniture and then measure for the rug sizes that will work. If you have no furniture yet, chalk mark its future position on the floor.

Investing in rugs. The money you spend on carpeting is almost completely nonrecoverable. While it is true that an attractive home is more easily sold than an unattractive one, carpeting is not the only way to make your home attractive. And the prospective buyer's tastes may differ from yours.

Rugs, on the other hand, are transportable and easily negotiable. The value of a good, well-cared-for rug does not drop.

A rug purchased from a reputable dealer cannot be resold to that or any other dealer for the same price. But you will not have any trouble selling the rug to a private individual at a price not far from the original. Certainly you will be able to recover far more than if you had put your money in carpeting. There will come a time when the value of a high-priced, well-main-tained rug will increase to its original price or more. So if you are planning to spend a bundle on a top grade, machine-made rug, go a bit further and buy a handmade rug. You will have secured an heirloom for yourself—one that will always be worth money, and there is also the pleasure of owning something of genuine beauty.

Antique rugs. Welcome to the thieves' market! Antiquing handmade rugs is almost as ancient an art as weaving them. All sorts of methods are used to "age" the rugs: They are left on public sidewalks so that passersby can wear them down and the sun can bleach their colors. They are washed and rewashed a dozen times. Even the experienced sometimes get taken by these ruses.

TYPES OF RUGS AND CARPETS

Rugs and carpets (the words are interchangeable in speaking of material and construction) are a kind of fabric. They are woven either by hand or by machine, from natural and synthetic fibers. Ordinary fabrics are woven from two sets of fibers: The "warp" runs the length of the cloth; the "woof" runs across. Rugs and carpets have a third set of fibers as well. These form the pile, the soft fibers projecting up from the base. To make the pile thick and soft, hundreds of short fibers have to be fastened side by side to the backing formed by the warp and woof. This is what makes rugs and carpets so much more expensive than flat fabrics. (Plush and velvet are actually rug or carpeting fabrics; they, too, have pile.)

Many kinds of fibers are used in making rugs, and there are several basic construction techniques.

The quality of a rug depends on the materials used, the quantity of material used, and the method of construction.

Materials. The natural rug materials include wool, silk, cotton, and jute. The naturals are not as strong as the synthetics, are subject to mildew and rot, and the wools can be destroyed by moths if not mothproofed. On the other hand wool will not burn by itself and none of the naturals produce particularly poisonous fumes when they do burn.

Wool. Wool is the strongest, most resilient and beautiful of all the natural fibers. It is lustrous, durable and soft. It takes most color dyes beautifully and retains them for ages. Without question the most beautiful rugs are made of wool. They are also the warmest, and produce little static electricity.

On the negative side, some people are allergic to wool. It must be mothproofed and is easily damaged by alkalies, such as human or animal urine. New rugs tend to shed a little and "pill," or form little balls. And wool costs more than all the other fibers used for rug making except silk.

You can identify wool by its distinctive odor when wet. Another test is to put a strand to a match flame. Wool will burn slowly, smell like burning hair (which it is) and sputter. Remove the flame and the wool stops burning. The ash is dark gray or black.

When rayon is mixed with the wool, there is little sputtering, the burning is rapid, and the flame may be yellow. When the flame is removed, the mixed fibers will continue smoldering and there will be little ash.

Silk. Silk is sometimes added to wool to increase its luster, but it is rarely used for an entire rug because of its high cost. Some ancient rugs were made of pure silk, notably the oriental rugs of Qum.

Cotton. The better-woven rugs use cotton or silk threads for their warp and woof. Cotton pile rugs are only suitable for small throw rugs, like bathroom rugs, that need to be washed frequently.

Jute. This is the material from which burlap is woven. It is a strong, tough vegetable fiber, but very rough and harsh. It does not take stain well. Jute is mainly used for rug backing and mats. For these purposes it is excellent.

The synthetic rug materials are stronger, harsher to the touch, do not take color as well and fade more quickly than the naturals. They also produce much more static electricity when walked on.

Nylon. This is the number one synthetic; strongest and

most durable of them all, but most costly. It is tough, hard, shiny, and nonabsorbent. It resists rot, mildew, fungus, insects, many acids and most alkalies, which means it will not be harmed if a small child or pet has an accident on it. Nylon also resists bleaches and stain removers. *However,* these chemicals can remove the dyes from the nylon.

Nylon is moderately harsh underfoot, so it is not often selected for the bathroom or bedroom. It also produces the heaviest electrical spark when you walk across it in winter.

Nylon is not as easily ignited as rayon. When nylon burns it smells like sealing wax and drips white beads. Rayon can be set afire more easily. It will sustain fire and drip black beads.

Acrylic. This is a family of synthetics and includes modacrylics. Not as strong nor as soil resistant as nylon, they are most often used with other synthetics as a fire retardant. The only advantage besides price and reduced inflammability that the modacrylics have over nylon is their reduced sensitivity to sunlight. They will not lose color at the same rate as nylon in bright sunlight.

There is no certain, simple way of identifying an acrylic other that it will not burn and melt as readily as the other synthetics. Unfortunately for identification, the degree of difference depends on how the acrylic has been treated. Acrilan, Creslan, and Orlon are the better known trade names of acrylic fibers.

Polyester. This man-made fiber is fairly stain resistant, holds onto bright, clear colors well and is bulky, which gives it a luxurious appearance. In bright colors these fibers do not hide soil very well, and they are less wear resistant than nylon and acrylics. Famous trade names in this group include Kodel, Dacron III, Encron, and Fortel.

Polypropylene. This group includes the olefins, of which Herculon and Marvess are the better known trade names. They are the most stain resistant of all the plastic fibers. They are generally first choice for places where food may be spilled—

kitchens, playrooms, etc. They do not have the "woollike" appearance of the other synthetics, and while they are long-wearing, they do have very low melting points. You can leave a burn line by quickly dragging your heel over the surface. They are generally used for hard-finish, closely-woven rugs, with a short pile, that is usually looped.

CONSTRUCTION

The quality, beauty, and longevity of a rug depends to a great extent on the method of weaving.

Hand weaving. Warp and woof threads are strung over the loom. The size of the loom determines to a great extent the size of the rug to be woven. The weaver hand ties short pieces of thread to the warp and woof threads. Each piece is knotted in place. There may be as few as 200 knots to the square foot, but professional rug weavers make as many as 17,424. (The Agrippa rugs of India, distributed by the Pande, Cameron Co. of New York, have this many knots.) The pile may extend out any distance from ½ inches to several inches.

Oriental rugs. An oriental rug is a rug with hand-knotted pile, (usually) hand-made in Asia. There are said to be over 440 different types.

A hand-tied Oriental rug.

You can recognize a handmade rug by looking first at its back. You cannot see the knots from this side, but you can see the pattern, because the pile threads run all the way through, and you can see the loops of wool that have been wrapped around the woof threads. Now, look at the front or top of the rug. Push the pile threads to one side. Look deeply and closely and you will see the knots.

Once you have seen the front and back of a handmade rug you can always distinguish it from one machine-made.

Machine weaving. When a machine-woven rug is made as thick and as lush as a handmade rug, the same high-quality wools and cottons are used, and the same care is taken in dyeing and designing, the machine-woven rug can almost be as beautiful as the handmade rug. But the hand-woven rug will always look different, and, most people believe, more beautiful. Its many small variations, and the thin line of differing color that encloses the pattern elements, give a handmade rug an individuality and visual depth a machine-made product never achieves.

The chances that you will be faced with this decision are fairly slim. Machine rugs are made to sell at a lower price and are not usually as thick and luxurious as the handmade. This difference is immediately obvious.

Tufting. This is the least expensive and least desirable way of making rugs. Because it is inexpensive 80% to 90% of all rugs sold are made this way.

Pull apart the strands to find the knots in a hand-tied rug. It's especially easy with shag, since its long strands are relatively wide spaced.

You can recognize a handmade Oriental rug by looking at its back. While you cannot see the knots on this side, the pattern will be visible because the pile threads run all the way through.

The back of a patterned machine-made rug.

In tufting, pile threads are looped through the backing and out again. But there is no knotting. Instead, the back of the rug is covered with a layer of latex (liquid rubber), which solidifies and holds the pile threads in place.

We feel this method of construction is satisfactory for carpeting, but not for rugs. Carpets are stationary and even when the rubber backing deteriorates the piling remains in place. However, if you move an old rug made by this method, and happen to bend the rolled rug sharply in the process, you may rip it at the bend or at the least loosen some of the rubber and cause the rug to shed.

However, a rubber-backed throw rug on a bare floor may be highly desirable even though it will be comparatively short-lived. The rubber backing keeps the rug from slipping, which is an important advantage.

Tufted rugs do not contain as much fiber as hand-woven or machine-woven rugs and therefore do not wear as long, are not as beautiful, but are less expensive.

Needle punching. This is a variation of the tufting method. Tufting is accomplished by dozens of machine-driven needles working simultaneously. Needle punch is done with a single needle. Tufting produces single-color and large-pattern rugs and carpeting. Needle punching is used to produce detailed designs. A needle-punched rug is almost always a custom-designed rug.

Like tufted pile, a needle punched rug is held in place with latex on the back of the rug, not by knots. Therefore you can always recognize tufted- and needle-punched rugs by noting this latex backing. In some instances the back of the rug is covered by a smooth layer of burlap. Since this is never done with any other type of rug, you know you have a tufted- or needle-punched rug in hand.

The quality of the latex applied to the back of a rug has a direct effect upon the life of that rug. When pure latex is used, the rug will hold together 10 to 20 years. When a large percentage of clay is mixed in with the latex, the backing tends to crack rapidly as it ages. Unfortunately there is no simple way to determine just how much the latex has been adulterated, if at all.

CARPET TILES

Carpet tiles are sold in various fibers and weaves and in sizes ranging from 8- to 12-inch squares. The backs of these tiles are covered with an adhesive. Pull the protective paper away, press the tile into place and you have "a tough, beautiful, permanent carpet," the ad says. Since this is a do-it-yourself product needing little skill, many people have purchased and installed carpet tiles.

Where the traffic is light and no liquids are spilled, these tiles will remain in place for a number of years. Where traffic is heavy and liquids do get spilled, the tiles tend to pick up fairly soon. No matter how carefully you install them, liquids can seep under the tiles, and they loosen and curl. Once that happens you can try glueing them down again with rubber cement, but it rarely works well.

Another reason for not purchasing and installing carpet tiles is that very often a one-piece carpet of the same quality costs no more than the tile, and will stay on the floor better.

It would be unfair to leave the subject without mentioning that tiles will stay down if you don't clean them very often. If you have a sun parlor or a similar room where there is little traffic, tiles are reasonably practical. Unfortunately, most people put carpet tiles down in kitchens and playrooms, where they do not remain in place very long.

TEXTURE

Broadloom. This term merely refers to the width of the carpet. It has nothing to do with its quality. Today, broadloom carpet can be had in rolls as wide as 18 feet or even wider.

Sculptured. The surface of the rug is cut down in various places to carve or "sculpture" the rug's surface. Beautiful and expensive when done by hand. Not so beautiful and a lot less expensive when done by machine.

Axminster. Axminister, Wilton, and velvet are types of weaves and are specific loom terms. All you need know about them is that Axminster is woven in what might be termed one direction. Pieces of this carpeting cannot be laid indiscriminately but must all have the weave running in the same direction.

Velvet. Also called plush, cut pile, frieze, and splush. It has the same texture as is produced by hand weaving. All the fibers rise vertically from the surface of the backing. All the fibers are parallel and all the fiber ends are cut to the same length to provide a flat surface. Footprints produce shadows, and if you run your hand across the pile the color will appear different.

Random shear. Some of the fibers rise straight out of the backing and are cut, the rest are looped. Most of the fibers are of the same height so that a flat surface results. This texture stands up to traffic much better than velvet.

Two-level loop. By varying the heights of the cut and uncut or looped fibers, various surface patterns are produced in the surface of the pile. This type of weave stands up to traffic as

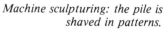

Machine sculpturing: the pile is shaved in patterns.

well as random shear, and the two levels add visual interest.

One-level loop. Of all the textures this is the most resistant to traffic and soiling. The loops are low, and tightly woven to exactly the same height. Traffic tends to slide more easily over this carpet surface than any of the others. This is first choice for commercial establishments, indoor/outdoor carpeting, stairs, and wherever else you can expect a lot of action.

Shag. Perhaps the popularity of shag has waned. We hope so. At one time shags could be purchased with individual fibers as much as 6 inches long. The original intent, according to the advertisements, was to produce a grasslike appearance.

Shag is made like velvet. Each individual fiber originates at the backing and is cut to any desired length. Shag is far easier and less expensive to manufacture than velvet; perhaps that is why it was pushed so strongly. The length of the fiber tends to hide the fact that there is a limited number of them.

Deep shag needs a special vacuum attachment, since the fibers are pulled into the cleaner by the normal power brush. It will not stand up to any kind of traffic, it tends to get caught on shoes, and the threads pull out. It cannot and should not be used on stairs. The backing shows through at the bends, and it can trip anyone coming down the steps.

PADDING

No rug or carpet should ever be placed directly on a floor. Without padding underneath, shoes grind the rug or carpet directly against the unyielding floor. No matter how high-quality the rug or carpet may be, it will not last long without adequate padding.

People who have antique and otherwise valuable rugs put a pad *and* another rug or carpet under the valuable rug. Some owners of priceless rugs make their guests remove their shoes before walking on them. The beautiful oriental rugs in the mosque in the Dome of the Rock in Jerusalem are protected this way. The rugs are piled several deep and the millions of faithful and curious who enter must remove their shoes.

Waffled urethane protective rug pad.

The small throw rugs placed directly in front of an entryway are there for the express purpose of picking up soil. Having no pad under them ensures that they will better remove the soil from the shoes that tread on them. These rugs are not expected to last long. They should be washed frequently; when they are soiled they no longer protect.

Hair, latex, synthetic foam, sponge, and jute are used for pads. Thick, heavy paddings are best, although some people do not like too much bounce. Test the pad in combination with the carpet you select before buying. You should at least be satisfied with the feel underfoot.

Cushion-backed carpeting. Some carpeting is made with a fairly dense rubber pad permanently fastened to its underside. It is not necessary to purchase and fit a pad. Some of this combination carpeting is so thick and stiff you don't have to fasten it to the floor in as many places as carpeting with separate padding. But wherever the edges of the combination carpeting are exposed to traffic, they should be fastened down.

When the carpet is made wholly of synthetic materials and its permanent backing is made of real or synthetic rubber, both can withstand moisture to a high degree. This is a good choice, therefore, for basements and the like where there may occasionally be some water seepage.

Another plus on the side of cushion-backed carpeting is that the backing provides dimensional stability. These carpets do not readily wrinkle or stretch; neither will their edges unravel, so there is no need to bind them.

Hair padding. Curled horsehair, locked in a thin coating of latex, is considered to be the best all-around pad. It is flexible, stands up well to time, doesn't block heat as much as other types of padding and most of all permits a maximum amount of air to pass up and through the carpet, helping to keep it dry. Dryness is a must for all rugs and carpeting containing natural fibers.

Sponge padding used to be made from natural rubber. Now it is made from synthetic rubber or one of the plastics. It has lots of spring, but little body. If you want a lot of bounce, this is the one to choose. Because it has little body, it does not last as long as other types of synthetic foam padding.

Plastic foam. The best is made from urethane, in various weights ranging from 3 pounds per cubic foot to 6 pounds per cubic foot. The better pads are the heavier pads, in density, not dimension, but even the heaviest padding should not be less than ½ inch thick. The waffled shape is considered to be a little better than flat shapes because it can pass a little air. Like all synthetics, urethane foam is insect- and mildew-proof.

Jute and hair. This is not a desirable padding. The better mixtures are the ones with more hair and less jute. Of course, the thicker they are the better. Since jute and hair are natural fibers, watch out for moisture, which will cause mildew and attract insects.

Jute. This padding material is last on the list. It tends to come apart, attract insects and break down more quickly than any of the others. But it is still far better than nothing at all. If you have spent almost all your money on the rug or carpet, at least get a jute pad.

No padding material is any good if it is paper thin. The pad breaks down in high traffic areas. Wear on the carpet or rug is then accelerated at this spot and the backing will show through more quickly than if no pad at all were used.

Pad the steps. Steps must also be padded. Use either single step pads, folded over the noses of each step, or a continuous padding running over the entire step assembly.

LAYING WALL-TO-WALL CARPETING

Carpet can be glued down. This method is generally limited to commercial establishments. It can be tacked down with carpet tacks. Or tackless fasteners can be used. These are strips of metal with tacklike projections facing upward. The carpet is pressed down against the tack points. Years ago, joints in carpets were sewn. Today they are joined with two-sided adhesive tape.

Doing it yourself. There is nothing terribly difficult about laying a carpet. Still, a certain amount of experience and knowledge is required. If you are determined to do this yourself, purchase the proper tools and spend some time studying the various how-to books available on the subject. A first-time, no-preparation go at it can easily make an expensive carpet look shabby. So take care or hire an experienced carpet layer.

How much do you need? In the case of a rug, measure the area you would like your rug to cover. Write down these dimensions. Then measure the minimum and maximum size of the areas you can possibly accept. Write down all these figures.

In the case of carpeting, make a drawing of the room that is to be covered, including all the dimensions. Bring this with you. Having it on hand will help you avoid waste and prevent the dealer from selling you more carpet than you need.

The shape of some rooms will force you to buy more carpet than you need. There may be no alternative to this, except to switch to a rug for that room. With the sketch and dimensions in hand all these things are easy to visualize; working from memory the best of us become confused.

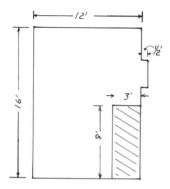

*Two ways to measure a room for carpeting. **A** uses one piece of thirteen-foot-wide carpeting (208 square feet); **B** is more efficient, using two pieces of eight-foot carpeting, or 172 square feet.*

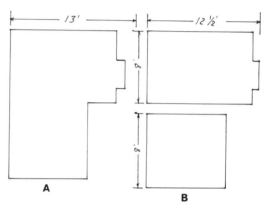

Use the same sketch to figure the number of square yards you may need. Multiply length in feet by width in feet to get square feet and divide by nine to get square yards. If you run into inches convert all the dimensions to inches and then divide by 1296. This is a lot easier than working with fractions of feet, especially if you have a pocket computer.

If the floor has alcoves and other odd shapes, break each down into simple rectangles and squares. Compute each separately, then add the total. This will give you the total area, but remember, you may have to purchase more than this to avoid extensive cutting and patching.

Stairs are measured differently. The rule of thumb is to allow ¾ yard or 27 inches of carpet length for every step. Check staircase width before ordering.

Some homeowners add an extra fold or two of carpeting at the foot of the stairs. Then when the carpet becomes worn, it is all loosened, and the carpeting pulled farther upstairs. When the carpet is replaced, the worn portions that covered the toes of the steps are now neatly folded out of sight inside the corners. This works if you do not wait too long and if the depth and height of the step permits it, and if you do not find the extra thickness at the bottom step objectionable, it is worth the expense of trying it.

DEALING WITH THE DEALERS

Many dealers are honest. However, companies do change hands, so be cautious.

Come prepared. Read this book and others on the subject. Bring along your measurements. Decide what you want to spend. Be prepared to shop around. Prices do differ from store to store and you can often save quite a bit by looking. Don't rush. Better to miss out on a bargain than to get stuck.

Be prepared for the come-on, be prepared to have your choice switched, be prepared to be told your knowledge of rugs is faulty or that Mrs. Hoozits just bought this wonderful purple shag for her entire house including poolside, that whatever you thought you may have wanted you really did not want. As they used to say on Delancey Street, "Examine the merchandise." Look, touch, feel, read the labels, go from shop to shop, and learn. Then make your purchase. Remember, you are not talking about a dollar and a half; you are considering a purchase that could be as high as several thousand dollars.

Final check list. Here's a summary of what you should check before you make your final selection.

Fold the carpet back. Fibers should be in even rows, firmly implanted.

Puffed and fluffy fibers indicate the fibers are soft and have little body. Hard, tightly twisted fibers last longer.

Compare fiber length and densities. Longer and denser ones are always better.

Examine backing. Is it tightly woven, hard and firm? It should be.

Ask for the weight of fiber or yarn. The salesman should know or should be able to get the information. Naturally, the heavier or more pile fiber, the better it will look and the longer it will last. Typically, nylon carpeting for residential use has a weight of 20 to 24 ounces. Commercial-grade nylon carpeting runs to 28 ounces and lasts several times longer.

Place the carpet or a portion of the carpet on the floor atop the padding you have selected. Stand on it. Walk on it. See how it feels. It should "give" generously, but not so much that you can feel the floor underneath.

Ask to see the Federal Trade Commission label. Every rug and carpet must have one. The label will state:

the manufacturer or distributor

the FTC registration number or manufacturer's name

the generic name of all fibers used

the percentage of each fiber used

the country of origin, if imported

Before you buy. Before you sign anything make certain you have the following in writing. No legitimate dealer will refuse to give it to you.

a copy of the information contained on the FTC label

weight of fiber; number of knots per square foot if hand woven

carpet color and its code number

whether or not it meets any inflammability tests

exact yardage of carpet to be delivered

exact yardage of padding

description of padding, material, thickness, etc.

full and total installation fee, if any; method of installation

whether or not installer will remove and dispose of old carpeting, if there is any

date of delivery and installation

guarantees, warrantees including terms for repair, replace-

*ment, cash refund, prorated refund; time period if any,
and*

*what extras may be charged, on what basis and the
maximum amount*

the full and total price

In addition, it is wise to take home a swatch of the carpeting and pad you selected, just to make certain there is no confusion in the shipping department. By matching the sample to the delivered goods you can be certain you are getting what you selected.

Signing. Take all the time necessary to read your sales agreement carefully. Have anything you don't understand spelled out. If anything has been left out, have the salesman or manager write it in.

Paying. Put down no more than a reasonable deposit—about 10%—until the rug or carpet is delivered and you have examined it thoroughly. Lay it out and look at every inch, front and back. We have seen more than one $5,000 rug with a hole in it. If installation is part of the deal, don't pay until the installation is completed to your satisfaction. If you are going to do the installation yourself, or have it done, make certain this does not negate your guarantee. If you have had to purchase more carpeting than you need, ask for the scraps. They belong to you and can be very useful.

If you let yourself get talked into paying when you sign for the rug, you have no recourse if you have to wait months for delivery or installation, receive the wrong merchandise, or if the carpet is badly installed.

If you can only buy the rug or carpet on an installment basis, think twice about making the purchase at all. If you can't pay all at once, borrow the money from a bank or credit card company, and pay cash when the merchandise is delivered. In this way you will keep the leverage to secure proper service. Once you sign the store's time payment plan, you owe the full sum and your only redress is to go to court in the event of a defect or mix-up.

CARING FOR FLOOR COVERING

Dirt, moisture, insects, and sunlight are the major enemies of rugs and carpets.

Use door mats outside your entrance doors and small, washable throw rugs inside the entry ways. Place rug runners over all carpeting and rugs that are in the normal traffic flow, particularly from the front and back doors. Plastic runners are not as good because they do not remove and hold dirt.

You may consider runners unattractive, and they are. But they can be removed and put away easily enough when you want your home to look especially nice.

The runners and throw rugs must be kept clean, otherwise the dirt they have picked up will be distributed inside your home.

Dirt on rugs and carpets can be cleaned with a vacuum cleaner. Most have two actions: a revolving brush to loosen the soil and a vacuum to suck it up. When cleaning a prized oriental or a beautiful machine-woven rug that is not very soiled, it is wise to disconnect the brush. Mild vacuuming is sufficient. Many people do not vacuum antique orientals at all; they brush them gently.

Beating rugs is a thing of the past. It just damages and weakens the rug.

Even a small quantity of moisture can ruin a good natural fiber rug or carpet in a few weeks. Therefore natural fiber rugs should never be placed directly on concrete, above or below ground. If you are going to put a natural fiber rug on a synthetic pad in a basement or cellar, make certain the concrete is perfectly dry. Natural fibers will absorb nearby moisture.

If a natural fiber rug should become wet or damp, lift it up by placing some old chairs or crates underneath. Arrange for air to flow over and under it. Use an electric fan if necessary. A wet or damp rug lying flat on a perfectly dry floor will take a long, long time to dry. During this time rot and mildew can set in, produce an odor and do some damage.

CLEANING

Washing. Both synthetic and natural rugs can be cleaned by washing them with mild soap and lukewarm water.

Small rugs can be washed in an extra-large washing machine. Take your rug to a coin-operated laundramat with 50-pound-capacity washers. If you can fold the rug in without damaging it; you can wash it. Just use lukewarm water and a little soap. Incidentally, you may be surprised by how large a rug you can fit into these machines; we get our 9 by 12 into one.

The alternative to washing the rug by machine is to do it by hand. You can do this on a clean driveway that is absolutely free of oil and grease, or on your lawn, if the grass is thick.

On the driveway, hose the drive generously, spread the rug, wet it down, apply soap and use a scrub brush if necessary. Then hose it free of all soap. After turning it over, lift it onto a number of boxes and chairs. Rain will do it no harm, but don't leave it out there until fall.

Do the same over grass, but if the grass is short, or there are bare spots, lift the rug onto boxes and similar supports.

Steaming. There are any number of compounds with which to clean carpets. Some you sprinkle on and just vacuum. Others require a carpet cleaning machine. The best is the steam cleaner. This sends a cloud of steam down into the carpet and at the same time vacuums the dirt up. With others, you only pick up the soil that adheres to the particles. The other soil sinks beneath the surface.

Rugs can be home-cleaned outdoors by scrubbing with a brush and soapy water.

Rinse off the soap with the garden hose.

Normally, carpets are not removed and cleaned, but we imagine there is no reason why this could not be done to synthetics, which would not shrink. Wools might.

Insects. Moths are of course the greatest danger, and they only attack wool rugs. If you keep your home screened, moth-proof your clothing, and hang mothballs in the closets, you will protect your wool rugs fairly well. It is not the moths that do the damage, but their larvae.

If you see a female moth flying about, destroy it. If you have your rugs commercially cleaned, have them mothproofed as well. If moths attack en masse, spray the room with an insecticide that will not stain or soil the rug; but don't soak the rug with it.

If you store the rug for the winter, add moth flakes before you roll it up and if at all possible, place it in a cloth or plastic bag that can be closed.

Sunlight. Direct sunlight fades just about all fabrics, including rug fabrics. Some of the synthetics fade more quickly than others, and most synthetics fade more quickly than wool. The only preventative is to close window shades. When this is not possible, move the rug about so that it at least fades evenly.

SPOT REMOVAL

The same methods used to remove spots from other fabrics should be used with carpets. The sooner it's done the better, and lift, never rub.

Pick it up. If the spot is a solid or a semisolid like butter, use a knife and carefully skim it from the surface of the carpet. With lots of care and a little luck you can pick up most of it this way.

If the spot is a liquid and you act fast, you can pick up most of it while it is still on the surface. Touch the tip of a clean piece of cotton cloth to the liquid. Even if it has been absorbed to some extent, you can still get some up this way. Be certain to use a clean cloth, or soil from the cloth may travel down to the carpet.

If the spot is an oil and it has seeped in to some extent, sprinkle an absorbent on top of it. The best absorbent is Fuller's earth, which you can find in many drug stores. Sprinkle it on, let it soak up as much soil as possible, then remove it with a vacuum cleaner holding the cleaner a little above the spot. DO NOT RUN THE CLEANER OVER THE SPOT! This can spread the soil. You can also pick up the absorbent carefully with a soft brush.

Cornstarch, French chalk, cornmeal, talcum powder and some of the commercial spot removers such as Carbona's Spray Spot Remover are also absorbents. With any of them you will have to make repeated applications. The Carbona contains an oil solvent which evaporates. The remaining powder is brushed away.

These steps may not remove all the spilled material. When they can do no more and the spot is an oil, you can use an oil solvent such as Carbona or a similar one, which contains tri-chloroethane or perchloroethylene. These solvents evaporate completely. Apply a few drops; let them soak in, then pick up with the tip of a clean, dry cloth. Repeat as often as necessary.

Do not use any of the combination spot removers such as Shout, K2-B, Magic Pre-Wash, and others. These contain soaps in addition to other chemicals. They will not evaporate completely, but must be washed out with soap and water.

Sticky spots. Lift as much as you can with a knife. Then wet with water and soak up the solution with a dry, clean cloth. Repeat as many times as necessary. If an oily residue remains— as it might from a milk or ice cream spill—try a little mild soap and lukewarm water. Follow with clean cool water. If this does not work, try the combination cleaners—Shout, etc. Be very cautious with wool. Test first on a hidden corner. Follow with a generous clean-water washing.

There is no harm to flooding the area with clean, cool water. Place several towels beneath the rug at the soiled area; pour the cool water on and let it flow through the rug into the towels. In a sense you are actually washing this portion of the rug.

Acids and alkalies. Pick up the spilled material as quickly as possible. If it is an alkali, like urine, wet down with cool water to which a few drops of lemon juice have been added. Repeat several times with plain water to make certain all the alkali has been removed or it will bleach the rug or carpet. Flood with clear water if necessary.

In the case of acid—vinegar, pickle juice, lemon juice, etc.—add a drop of ammonia to a quart or more of water and apply it first. Pick it up and follow with more clear water. Flood with clear water if you believe it is necessary.

Stains. These are the toughies. The trick is to remove the stain without removing the color from the rug, and that is difficult.

Start by removing all the oil and sugar that may have been the original cause of the spot. What will not come out is a stain; literally an unwanted dye. Now you have to use bleach, and use it with tremendous caution, or you will end up with a white spot.

Wet the area. Start with the weakest bleach in the list below. Wait and watch. If it works, start washing it out by flooding *before* it has completed its job. If it starts to bleach everything, flood immediately.

The bleaches are, in ascending order of strength,

>*white vinegar*
>*lemon juice*
>*hydrogen peroxide*
>*ammonia*
>*chlorine (Clorox)*

Use a dry bleach—Clorox II or Snowy—on synthetics. Use the other bleaches on wools. To weaken any of the bleaches, mix them with water. Apply any of the bleaches with great caution, preferably with an eye dropper. To make certain you will not produce a white spot immediately, try the bleach on a sample of the carpet or one fiber of a rug.

11

Think Used

There is a reluctance on the part of many people to purchase used or secondhand furniture. Many people who do because their budgets are limited rush to dispose of their old furniture as soon as they can.

The attitude that secondhand is somehow disgraceful is an error. A good piece of furniture is a good piece of furniture no matter how many changes of ownership it may have had. Would you discard a Louis XV settee merely because old Louis had owned it first?

THE REAL BARGAINS

Because of this attitude, the only furniture that is a real bargain is used furniture. Though furniture does not wear out like an automobile or TV set, it is "used" as soon as it leaves the dealer's showroom. Its price drops far more than the price of a used automobile. New furniture drops 50% or more the moment it is delivered to the buyer.

This price drop is due partly to the vanity of the general public and partly to the high markup on furniture.

USED CAN BE BETTER THAN NEW

Every age that has seen furniture has had its three levels of furniture quality. On the lowest level there is minimum furniture made as quickly and as cheaply as possible. There is middle-quality furniture, which can be graded as "moderately good" to "excellent." And there is the best, made of solid select woods, by master craftsmen working according to designs of noted furniture designers.

Today, pricing is ambiguous. Some junk is relatively expensive, and middle-quality pieces approach top-quality pieces in prices.

When you go back fifty or so years, medium-priced furniture was of good quality; much of it would fall into our present-day top level. One reason was that manufacturers did not have the materials and machines to make low-quality products that looked good.

Thus when you look at what a middle-income family of the 1920s might have purchased, you are looking at a piece of furniture a high-income family of today might not be able to afford. This writer remembers well the many couches and settees upholstered in leather and stuffed with horsehair that were unceremoniously dumped on the sidewalks in his hometown for the trash collector. Cloth was the "in" upholstery material at the time, so leather furniture was discarded.

Material. Since lumber was far less costly years ago, older pieces of furniture usually contain more wood in thicker and stronger parts. Also, more of the harder, stronger woods were used because they were more readily available and because the old furniture makers depended more on glue and joints than on metal fasteners.

You will also find far less plywood used in the old pieces, and more solid (not veneered) pieces of beautiful wood. Although veneer can be beautiful, a solid piece of wood has a charm that no veneer can duplicate.

A prize in used furniture—a 1900 circular china closet in good condition.

More screws were used in the old furniture, and more braces and supports. The old drawers had two or more slides, unlike many of those in modern furniture, which have only one or none.

Labor. Since labor was more available in the years gone by, a higher percentage of the used pieces will be carved to some degree; there is more ornamentation, more curves, bends, and parts. Usually the extra hand labor added to the attractiveness of the furniture.

HOW MUCH IS IT WORTH?

Always much less than new. As a general rule you should not pay more than 25% of what a comparable new piece would fetch in a store. The used piece may have begun life as a far more desirable piece of furniture, with better wood, greater detail, and better design. But it *is* used, it has to be hauled home and most likely it needs a little cleaning and touching up.

Don't get carried away. The only way you will know whether an asked price is reasonable or not is to go armed with information. The fact that it is old does not make it particularly valuable, and purchasing old furniture to hold until the pieces become antiques is a very specialized business. Study this book and others on furniture. Look at the furniture offered for sale in the stores, read the used-furniture ads, look at lots of used furniture and note its price. If you are not prepared to do this you are buying blind, and will be better off to go to a reputable store and buy new merchandise. It doesn't take as much knowledge and experience to buy used furniture without getting stuck as it does to buy a used car, but it does take some.

CONDITION

In giving you a rule-of-thumb price guide we have assumed the furniture to be in reasonably good condition. This means, that all you need do is wipe the piece clean with a damp cloth, that there may be a few nicks and scratches but that you can live with them. When anything more needs to be done you had best stop and think carefully.

Surface defects. If the piece has been varnished and the varnish has worn through at spots, it is a relatively simple matter to refinish them so long as the exposed wood has not been affected. If the wood has been affected, the problem becomes more complex. If the wood was stained and the stain worn through, you now have to restain the spot. If the wood has been soiled to the point where soap and water will not bring it back to its original color, you most likely will have to sand the soil away, fill the area with molten shellac, sand again and refinish.

If there are dents in the surface they have to be filled with stick-shellac. This is not too difficult for the beginner, but it does take some practice and some skill at matching colors.

If the veneer is loose along the edges and you can, with your hand, press the veneer smoothly back in place, it is no problem to glue it back down. If the veneer bulges in the center of the piece, the task is difficult. In some instances, drying will flatten the veneer. More often a section has to be cut out, glue applied and the section replaced. As you can imagine, this requires considerable care and some experience.

If the piece has been painted and some of the paint has been chipped off, you can spot-paint, but the results will rarely be good. You will have difficulty matching the faded old paint.

Stripping. If the piece is sound but its finish is not good, it must be completely refinished. There are two ways to do this, but don't rush in either direction.

Imagine you are constructing a piece of furniture and have to glue together several pieces of wood for a part of it. If you simply varnish over the pieces, the joints will be visible. So you "glaze" it—you cover it with a thin coat of paint, and then varnish the piece. Sometimes this was done to simulate wood of another color. When you strip this part of the furniture, all the sins come to light. Before you refinish you have to reglaze; this can be highly skilled work, so proceed cautiously.

You can strip furniture yourself. It is not difficult. Or you can pay to have the job done. A piece like a chair will easily take a gallon of paint remover and at least a half day's work. A stripper, who pours the remover on with a hose, can do a much better job in far less time. It would be foolish to suggest any price here, but you can see sample pieces in his shop and estimate the cost of stripping your piece that way. (Note that some strippers use an alkali that bleaches the wood. Check their method, as the bleaching may require sanding.)

You can find the names and addresses of furniture strippers in the phone book, or by asking at antique shops and second-hand furniture stores.

Refinishing. Once the wood has been stripped clean and prepared for finishing, it is fairly easy to do either a varnish or paint job with spray cans. You will need three or four cans per chair to do a good, solid job, with a reasonably thick coat of paint or varnish.

An alternative is to hire the stripper or a furniture refinisher to do the job for you.

In either case, you can see that the expenditure is considerable. Decide whether the used piece is worth it.

Deep gouges. The only way these can be repaired is by filling them with stick shellac. This is not at all expensive, but it does require some skill and a good eye. And it is not easy to make a color match so close it cannot be seen. You can get an estimate from a refinisher if you are planning to purchase a used piece and do not want to repair the dents and gouges yourself.

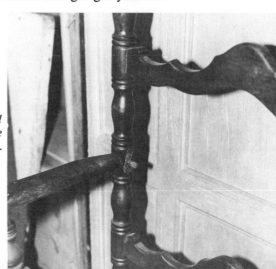

This used chair, in otherwise good condition, has a missing back piece that will be very hard to replace.

Missing veneer. When a piece of veneer has broken off and is missing, the task of replacing that piece and making it all look like new is not a job for a beginner. Get an estimate on the repair before you make the purchase. Work like this can run into hundreds of dollars, depending on the extent and difficulty of the work. You cannot plan on removing the rest of the veneer and using the furniture that way. The veneer was installed to hide unattractive wood or joints. Without it, the piece will be ugly.

Loose frame, loose joints. Most table legs are bolted in place and can be tightened by turning the nut on the bolt. It is also an easy matter to tighten wood screws. But most chairs are held together with glued joints. To retighten a glued joint properly it must be taken apart. This is only easy when *all* the joints will come apart. It is difficult to take tight joints apart without damaging the piece. You may be able to force glue into a loose joint without taking it apart, but this is not usual. Unless you are prepared to go to a lot of trouble or the repair is obvious, a used piece of furniture with loose glued joints isn't worth much.

Cracks and splits. If the crack or split is long and you can push the parts together without difficulty, you should have no trouble making a repair. If the crack is across a specific part and short, as for example across a leg, there is little chance that a strong repair can be made, even with the best glue or cement.

Missing pieces. If the missing parts are knobs, pulls and the like you can purchase a whole replacement set. You won't be able to match the originals.

Warped furniture. Sometimes warpage is so bad that the piece looks crooked; at other times the only things affected are doors and drawers that will not close or that stick. If the warpage is very bad, chances are that nothing will ever straighten the wood. If the warpage is slight and the furniture has been stored in a damp place, there is a possibility (*only* a possibility) that it will straighten itself when it dries out—a process that can take months. However, if the piece is warped and has been in a very dry place for a long time, even if the warpage is small, there is little chance that it will correct itself with time or that you can correct it by applying pressure. The warp is almost permanent.

Woven seats and backs. The woven sections of damaged furniture can be repaired, but the amount of labor involved varies greatly from one type of woven seating to another. When the weaving material is coarse, like splint and sea grass, the work is simple and can be done by anyone without previous experience. When machine-woven cane has been used, all that is necessary is to remove the spline holding the cane in place and install a new sheet of machine cane. This can be done in an hour or two even by the inexperienced. But when the cane is hand woven, hours are required, even for the experienced. There are shops that do caning and chair weaving.The work cannot be inexpensive because of the labor involved. (Chapter 17 contains instructions for recognizing the various seating weaves and replacing some materials.)

WHAT USED FURNITURE NOT TO BUY

Stay away from stuffed furniture unless it is in excellent condition and can be used as is. Upholstering is expensive and in most cases represents the greater portion of the original cost. You can do your own upholstering and there are a number of books on the subject, but remember that a damaged piece of upholstered furniture, is worth little more than the value of its frame.

If the upholstery is excellent but a little soiled or faded, you might consider using it with a permanent cover. Don't imagine you can dye the faded portion to match the rest, and don't think that a really soiled spot is going to respond to any spot remover, though a light stain may.

You will come across many beautiful old pieces with torn and worn upholstery and beautifully carved frames that unfortunately have been cracked in several places. Unless you consider the piece so beautiful that you are willing to spend more to repair it than you would for a new one, keep your pocketbook snapped tightly shut, or you will be wasting your money.

Stuffed furniture also makes a good home for insects. If it comes from a commercial warehouse or any other dry and food-free place, there is little chance that it is buggy. Bugs need water and some kind of food. If it comes from a home where there might have been infestation, we suggest you pass it up, even if it is in excellent condition.

Should you want to be certain the piece you purchase is bug-free, place it on your driveway or in your garage, with plenty of open space around it, then spray it. Modern insecticides will destroy all insects quite thoroughly. Do not bring the piece into a small apartment. You could soon have an infestation even though you sprayed quickly and thoroughly.

Stay away from mattresses as well, unless you know who has owned them. They harbor not only insects, but pathological bacteria.

12

Antique Furniture

There are enough existing books about antique furniture to fill a fair-sized library. Yet we believe the information that follows to be more important to a *furniture buyer* than all of them.

AGE IS NOT ENOUGH

The general definition of an antique is anything more than one hundred years old. (Some exuberant dealers claim a mere fifty years is sufficient to "antique" a piece of furniture; but no one pays them much mind.)

Age versus value. We have before us, in our imagination, a plain deal table, unvarnished and simple, such as was common in American kitchens fifty and more years ago. The shopkeeper says, and we believe him, that the table is seventy-five years old. Across the room there is a second, almost identical table, which the dealer says and can prove is one hundred years old. Is the second table, the antique, worth more than the first—the used table? Perhaps a few dollars extra, but nothing more. AGE ALONE IS NOT WORTH ANYTHING. Bear that in mind when a seller ups the price on the basis of age alone.

Age versus beauty. Assume again for the sake of discussion that you are offered an attractive, used coffee table in good condition for $100. Or you can purchase an antique coffee table, also in good condition but that you consider ugly, for the same price. There is no contest. Why put something in your home that is unsightly merely because it is old? UGLY IS UGLY NO

MATTER HOW ANCIENT. Unless the ugly piece has some special story connected to it (that can be authenticated), or is so old and rare that even a chip is valuable, it is junk. You should pay no more than a "junk" price for it.

Condition is most important. So far as we are concerned, a few small chips and cracks in an old but beautiful piece don't make it unacceptable. We would still place it in our home and treasure it. However, chips, cracks, loose veneer, etc., have a tremendous negative effect upon the price of furniture. Up to a point, and this point takes a bit of explaining.

A Louis XIV bureau in good or better condition will fetch thousands of dollars at any auction. The same bureau in poor condition will be lucky to go for one tenth of the figure. No one would place a deteriorated piece of once beautiful furniture in their home; they would have it restored first, and that could cost thousands of dollars.

On the other hand, a Venetian armoire that didn't have worm holes, small splits, dents, and other defects would be suspect. All really ancient wooden furniture (from the Middle Ages and beyond) is in poor condition. In addition to the ravages of time, the ancient cabinet makers didn't do too good a job in smoothing boards and finishing them off.

So the word *condition* must be qualified by the age of the piece and its original appearance. The better its original condition and the closer to our own time it was made, the better its condition must be to be acceptable.

Damaged antiques. When a piece is old, beautiful and in excellent condition it is worth at least as much as an equivalent brand-new piece. Generally, it will sell for several times the price of an identical or nearly identical new piece of furniture. Damaged, the piece is hardly worth anything.

Since a cabinetmaker's time is costly, and a restorer's several times higher than that of a cabinetmaker, repairing a damaged antique can be extremely expensive. In some cases you can make an acceptable repair yourself in a reasonable length of time. In others, the defects may not bother you. A lot depends on the piece and what is wrong.

For example, Wedgewood china with a chipped edge is worth only pennies. But, depending on where the chip or chips are positioned, it may be possible to hang the china so that the support clips cover the defects. You then have a beautiful wall decoration, even though its intrinsic value is nil.

The point made here is that DAMAGED ANTIQUES MAY BE ACCEPTABLE IF THE PRICE IS LOW ENOUGH. But do not expect to resell damaged antiques at a profit. You never will unless you can restore them expertly.

A VERY SPECIALIZED INVESTMENT

There are any number of books on the subject of investing in antiques. They give examples of the rise in the overall price of antiques over the past few years, and the profits individuals have made by buying antiques. The stories are endless, just as are the stories of those who purchased Polaroid stock when it was first issued. And they are all true.

Equally true are the stories of the dealers who made even larger fortunes buying and selling antiques and the millions of people who are still anticipating the money to be made on the antiques they have bought. These stories have yet to reach print.

Today's young furniture designers charge outrageous prices for their work. You start at a financial disadvantage when

Pine and oak writing cabinet with satinwood marquetry, England, 1770-1775.

Hand-carved chair arm, England, 18th century.

you purchase it with the thought of eventual resale. None of them will ever achieve fame in the sense of a Chippendale or Hepplewhite. Modern designers are too commercial; produce too many copies of each design and are not known to the public. And none of us are going to live long enough to profit by any price rise in their furniture.

So to make a profit in antiques one must compete with others for the existing pieces, and there we are at a double disadvantage. Professional antique dealers haunt all the auctions, visit all the backcountry junk shops and their like, and spend most of their time at it. They have a tremendous knowledge of the subject. *And* they have a place from which to sell and a list of customers whose tastes and desires they know.

We are under still another handicap. You and I can never get as much for a piece of furniture when we sell it from our home as when a dealer sells an identical piece from his shop, and if we sell to a dealer we would get comparatively little.

Time and tide are against us. If you are still prepared to invest in antiques, remember that if inflation continues at the present rate, our dollar will lose half its real value in seven years. Thus, to break even, your antique must appreciate an equal amount. But there are the additional expenses of insurance, a bill of sale, and an appraisal, and the risk of normal wear and tear in your home. If you invested in tax-free bonds you would easily earn enough to offset inflation without half as much risk.

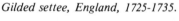

American Federalist rolltop desk, upper shelves missing.   *Gilded settee, England, 1725-1735.*

WHEN ANTIQUES ARE BARGAINS

We have a rolltop oak desk. It is a little more than a hundred years old. It is in good, but far from excellent, condition; it has been in use every day of its existence. A museum piece it will never be. A recent ad for a new rolltop desk of equal shape and size, made of pine, quoted $800. If we were in the market for a rolltop desk at this time we would happily pay $800 for an old oak desk and even go to $1,000 or perhaps $1,200 if it was like the one we have.

The oak desk will outlast the new one, despite its present age. Its value will not depreciate. The pine will not hold its price. It will be a century or more before it is worth the equal of a new desk then, and being made of softwood, we doubt that it will last even half that long.

The point is that a real antique piece of furniture in good condition or better is usually a good choice over an identical new piece, as long as you do not pay too high a premium because it is antique, and do not consider it an investment.

Immeasurable value. Up to this point we have discussed antique furniture from the dollar point of view. This is only one aspect of antique furniture. There is no dollar yardstick by which to measure the pleasure and joy a beautiful piece of antique furniture brings by just gracing your home.

Gothic credenza (note the Gothic arch in the fretwork). French, late 15th century.

Daybed, U.S. Civil War period.

FAKES

Only the most ardent collector has any idea of how many Hepplewhites, for example, were made, how many still exist, etc. Not too many years back it was the custom to restore fine antique furniture by disassembling the piece and rebuilding a dozen others from the parts. Each new piece of furniture contained a part of the old, and was considered a "restored" piece.

So in addition to all the other pitfalls and traps that may beset the would-be investor in antique furniture, there is a very real and constant problem of fakes. It gives one something to think about!

14

Making Your Own Furniture

Furniture for royalty and the wealthy in times past was made by artists who had devoted most of their lives to acquiring the necessary skills and experience. But there is a wealth of attractive and even beautiful furniture that can be made by the semiskilled and even the unskilled on their first time around.

Hundreds of thousands of people are presently making their own furniture. It is the only way they can secure what they need at a reasonable cost.

THERE ARE MANY LEVELS OF FURNITURE TECHNOLOGY

A coffee table made of a polished zebra wood slab is, in its way, just as beautiful as a table with involved marquetry and hand-carved legs. The two are just different. And there are many, many furniture designs that may not be beautiful, but that are attractive and highly functional. Some rooms, like the children's bedrooms can very appropriately be furnished with simple, functional furniture.

Then there is furniture that is merely functional and very simple to make even for the rank beginner. For example, one can make tables, beds, armoires, etc. from plywood cut to size at the lumberyard. (We are presently working on a book that will tell how.) In addition to other materials ordinary woods can be used. Rattan furniture is very easy to make, even for a beginner. Still another material to consider is plastic pipe. Some commercial companies are beginning to use this material, which can be cut with a hacksaw, is joined with cement, and bends like rattan, with the application of a little heat. (We are working on a book on this subject, too.)

SECURING INFORMATION

In some of the larger cities you will find classes in woodworking, where you can build furniture while you learn. Many vocational and trade schools give night classes in woodworking for a small fee.

The libraries are filled with books on woodworking, finishing, tools and techniques, furniture repairs, and all levels of furniture making. Many people work in wood as a hobby. If you make the effort you may find a neighbor who is experienced this way and will help you get started.

Tools. Unfortunately good woodworking tools and a woodworking bench are not inexpensive. When you add power tools, a bill can run to a thousand dollars or more. However, these tools do last a lifetime, which means used woodworking tools are available at considerable savings. Or you may want to start by renting your power tools from a local Rent-A-Tool shop.

Unfinished furniture. This type of furniture, made generally of pine is sold in shops and through the mails. Many newspapers carry their ads. Generally, all you need do is a little assembling and finishing, meaning varnishing. And usually all you will need in the way of tools is a screwdriver. Some unfinished furniture is excellent, but much of it will just barely do the job because the parts are too thin and the wood too soft.

The savings possible by buying unfinished furniture are usually not great. We suggest you seriously consider used furniture in its place, because in many cases you will find yourself discarding the low-priced unfinished furniture long before it has fulfilled its function in your home. This is not so with good, used furniture. It is heavier and far tougher.

15

Where and How to Buy Furniture

By this point you should have a fairly good idea of what constitutes well-made furniture and what does not. You should also know what you wish to purchase, at least in general terms of function, overall size, and design. Your problem, and it is a problem for most of us, is how and where to get the most furniture for your money.

Start your search with this bit of truth stuffed in your wallet or written in the back of your checkbook. You will never secure the maximum possible amount of furniture for your money, no matter how hard you try unless luck does that job for you. It is impossible to cover all the sales in your county or state; it is impossible to be everywhere or even anywhere at just the right time. If you aren't careful, you will be misled in your ideas about price by so-called friends who will lie to prove their financial acumen. Some will tell you they paid more for their furniture to make you believe they exist on a higher strata than you. Others will reduce the figure to prove they are nothing less than brilliant when it comes to outsmarting the shops.

Remember that the figures others give you are meaningless. The price you have to pay for an item is its current market price. Yesterday's numbers are gone.

TIME AND EFFORT

You are not going to come even close to the best of all possible deals without expending time and energy in searching. To go to just one source and do the best you can is to take a gamble that you will most likely lose. You will end up paying top dollar or close to it. On the other hand if you really search there is a very good possibility you can cut your costs by 25% at a minimum. If you try very hard you may even be able to furnish your home beautifully for as low as *half* the going price.

The markup on furniture is the highest of any item sold today except for very low-priced jewelry. Part of this is due to the nature of the business. (The rest is due to greed.)

Most people do not purchase furniture more than once or twice in their lifetime, and then they buy a complete houseful. It is not like groceries or even automobiles, which are replaced every few years. So real furniture sales are far and few between.

Furniture transportation is difficult and costly. Each piece must be hand-carried into the truck at the factory, hand-carried into the warehouse, back into the truck and back out again when it is sold. Many reliable furniture dealers have furniture refinishers on their payrolls. These men follow the trucks to remove the inevitable scratches that result from handling during delivery. Furniture showrooms are large and expensive to maintain.

Thus the basic cost of selling furniture is high, which means the investment is high, which means the markup is high because just about every businessman or woman will add a percentage of the total cost.

So unless you go from shop to shop and compare prices, you are not going to save. And since furniture markups are very high, there is plenty of room for price reductions that can amount to thousands of dollars on a room or two of furniture.

Take your time, be prepared to look and look some more, take notes, and bring along a ruler. Prices depend somewhat on size and there is no point to pricing an item that is not the correct size for your needs.

WHERE TO BUY NEW FURNITURE

Run-of-the mill furniture shops. These carry low- to middle-priced furniture. Compared to large department stores and furniture chain stores their prices are lower. But you will have to examine their merchandise and decide whether their lower prices are for lower-quality goods. Very often this very inexpensive furniture is just a step above junk, and you would be better advised to decorate with good used furniture instead.

Furniture shops all deliver.

Top-grade furniture chain stores and department stores. These carry the so-called brand names in furniture, but since there are some 500 of them, it is hard to know which is a famous brand and which isn't. You will generally get better service in these stores, a higher grade of furniture (at higher prices), a better selection, and some so-called "designer" pieces (which means someone has designed these to put his or her name on them). If you are a name dropper, this may be worth something to you.

Top-level shops and department stores deliver and set up. This means they will bring the pieces into your home and position them where you ask.

The better companies guarantee their merchandise. If you have a complaint that cannot be rectified by a service visit—if, for example, the fold-out daybed no longer folds—they will return it to the manufacturer. Discount houses will tell *you* to return the piece to the manufacturer yourself—that's what a manufacturer's guarantee means.

Department stores, and possibly some of the larger furniture stores and chains, offer revolving credit. If you time your purchase you can get almost 60 days without interest. This is done by buying a day or two after the day your monthly statement is prepared. If, for example, your statement reads "as of June 5" and you make your purchase on the 6th or 7th, the charge will not be posted until sometime before the 5th of the following month. Then you get the usual 30 days on top of that.

Factory outlets. These are discount houses that purport to have some special and direct connection to furniture manufacturers. They do. They buy from them.

You will find them at the outskirts of town where rents are

lower. They usually further cut costs by limiting themselves to "plain pipe rack" displays. They do not have ornate showrooms, many of them, nor salespeople who know something about the merchandise. They have clerks who take orders.

Their prices can be lower, but don't assume that they are. And don't comparison shop these places, because the fact that a piece carries a name brand doesn't mean it is identical to a similar piece in a downtown shop. Manufacturers produce "special" lines for special customers like these.

The major advantage of a factory outlet or discount store is that they have the merchandise on the premises. Put your money down at the front desk and you can pick the piece up at the building loading dock. (Delivery is extra, as is bringing the furniture into your home.) Once you have placed the furniture on top of your car or in the rented trailer, it is all yours. If you have any arguments or complaints, take them up with the manufacturer. Should you find the piece too large, too small or entirely wrong for your home when you bring it inside, lots of luck! Many places have a positively-no-return policy.

However, discount houses, factory furniture outlets, and their like are excellent for simple, sturdy, plain pieces of furniture—bunk beds for the kids, study tables, work benches, etc. You can't go wrong with these so long as you make certain you have all the parts before you leave, and that the piece will fit your space. However, you must make certain that the furniture is strong, sturdy, and well built. No one is going to steer you clear of the junk.

Catalog showrooms. These are variations of factory-outlet operations. They differ only in that they offer their customers catalogs that you can take home and use to make your selections at leisure.

Mail-order furniture. You will find mail-order furniture ads at the back of family magazines, travel magazines, and similar publications. Since assembly and shipping is a large part of furniture costs, and wholesale and retail profits add their share, these mail-order companies can offer a lot for the money. The one problem is that it is difficult for most people to visualize a piece of furniture from a photograph. Neither do dimensions mean much to many people. So to be certain the furniture will be large or small enough, make a rough duplicate from a cardboard box or two.

Do not worry that a mail-order house will cheat you. The United States has the best mail-order laws in the world. Mail fraud is a federal offense. It carries a long jail penalty.

However, if the furniture turns out to be what you do not want, you are going to have to repack and reship it yourself—and pay the shipping cost. Do not return anything before securing written confirmation. Then be certain to insure it and pay for receiving a signed receipt in return. No one is going to cheat you deliberately, but it is easy for packages to get lost in a big company.

Designer galleries. There are a few galleries that display limited edition designer furniture. They are listed in the phone book. If you want the best or close to the best unique pieces, these are the places to visit. But the prices are also close to the best.

However, there are some galleries that exhibit the work of individual craftspeople on commission. Generally their commission is 50%. If you can deal with the craftsperson individually, there is obviously a savings.

Furniture factories. Many furniture factories are open weekends and sell to the general public at a figure well below retail. Generally they do not advertise, because that would make their wholesale customers very, very angry. You may find them by asking around or checking with the furniture factories within driving distance—look through the yellow pages or local business registry. It is well worth the time you may spend searching.

Individual craftspeople. There are literally thousands of people making furniture for their own pleasure and for an occasional sale. You can find them in any of several ways. Ask your local lumberyard for one that deals in fine hardwoods. Visit this yard and ask about craftspeople who make furniture to order. Or, visit the high schools and colleges that have woodworking classes. There you will find not only students, but craftspeople who make fine furniture and come to use the schools' expensive woodworking equipment.

Their prices are high, because they work with fine, expensive woods. But the results will be beautiful and you will get exactly what you want. It is from these craftspeople who enjoy working in wood that you will get the most for your furniture dollar.

Unfinished-furniture shops. These places specialize in low-cost, unfinished furniture. Some of it is very good, though plain. But much of it has been made from soft pine so it can be sold at a lower price. These pieces aren't strong, and you would do better to find an equivalent piece of used furniture. (Note that if you do not finish—varnish or paint—these pieces they will soon become permanently soiled.)

WHERE TO BUY USED FURNITURE

Auction houses. These range from world famous Christie's and Sotheby-Parke Bernet to Harold's Genuine Furniture Auction Rooms. Some are legitimate; the people are actually auctioning off something. But those that advertise "an auction always in progress" usually hold no auctions at all.

Visits to the famous auction rooms are interesting, educational and generally free and open to the public. While on occasion a piece of furniture or art object may go on the block for a few hundred thousand dollars, the average sale is fairly low. One auction house advertises that the price of the average item is around $200. You can pick up good furniture here at reasonable prices. You just have to know what you are buying and refrain from speculating.

Come early, or examine the catalogs, so you know what is being offered. Just be careful that your price is not pushed up by the auctioneer's shill, whom you will recognize as the one who always bids but never buys.

Few auction houses at the lower end of the financial ladder have daily auctions. You will find auctions listed in the newspaper. However, when there isn't an auction going on, the place is a regular used-furniture shop.

You cannot bargain at an auction, but you can make a bid on nonauction merchandise. You might say, "This is very nice, but to me it is not worth more than . . ." There is nothing wrong with this. Remember that the used-furniture dealer did the same when he bought the merchandise, and chances are that he is asking two or three times what he paid for it, so there is a fat margin for him to lower his price. So you will often do better here than at a higher-priced used-furniture shop.

There are also always a number of business auctions going on; to find out about them, contact the local sheriff's office and watch the business sections of your local papers. You may not be interested in bidding on a drill press or truck scales, but most companies have offices and offices have desks, chairs, other office furniture and often pictures, rugs, and residential furniture in their reception areas.

Be certain to find out how payment is to be made before you go to an auction. Some auctioneers demand cash, some will take checks. Usually unless the items run to hundreds of thousands of dollars, full and final payment is demanded at the close of bidding, and the buyer is responsible for hauling the purchase away.

Estate sales. When you or I sell furniture in our home, it is a moving sale; when the wealthy sell, it is an estate sale. The major difference is that an estate sale is conducted by an auctioneer. Here is where you will find top-level furniture, real antiques, and all that go to make a large home beautiful. You will also find a very knowledgeable, well-heeled group of experts bidding on the pieces offered. Since many are commercial buyers bidding for their shops and private clients, you can in some instances outbid them and still pay less by half for an item than you would in their shop.

However, you can also get stuck here. The fact that the

now deceased Mrs. Richbucks owned a piece doesn't guarantee its authenticity. In the arts the rich are taken more often than the poor.

Come early, look hard. Make cetain they will take your check before you even bother to go. It is always "let the buyer beware" at these auctions, and usually you must do your own hauling. But if top-level antiques and art at relatively reasonable prices are what you are after, estate auctions are worth attending.

Used-furniture shops. We mention this source following estate auctions because all used-furniture shops do not limit themselves to ordinary used furniture. As a general rule, their prices are among the highest of all sources of used furniture, and many do not deign even to use the term *used furniture*. (But that is what they carry!) These are the shops that send buyers to the estate auctions and often buy an entire household with one bid.

You will pay more for run-of-the mill used furniture in these places than at thrift shops and their like, but there are advantages. These places stock groups of items: tables with chairs, beds with dressers. All their stock is in one place, and you can inspect it all at one time. And they will usually deliver as part of the deal.

In addition, if you ask them, most of them will keep an eye out for what you may want that they do not have on hand.

You will find used-furniture shops in the older parts of a city.

Commission shops. These are shops at which people leave things to be sold at commissions ranging from 25% to 50%. They have medium- to high-quality furniture and bric-a-brac.

Their prices, generally higher than in thrift shops or Salvation Army depots, are based on the general pricing guides for used furniture, antiques and bric-a-brac, the condition of the piece and what the owner wants for it. They drop with the passage of time. One possible way to secure a better price is to make the shop owner an offer. If not authorized to take less, the owner will contact the person selling the furniture. Some will settle for a fast deal; others would rather wait. If you simply return to the shop again and again waiting for the price to drop, you will most likely arrive someday and find the item has been sold.

If you are seeking a compromise between going again and again to thrift shops and paying full price for something new, the commission shop is probably the best place to go. Most of them will take a self-addressed postcard and mail it to you when something you are looking for comes in. Sometimes they know what they will be receiving soon.

Generally, commission shops will take checks. Some know of local low-cost furniture haulers they can recommend. Incidentally, these are good places to sell *your* unwanted furniture.

Thrift shops. The Volunteers of America, the Salvation Army, and similar organizations operate thrift shops. Sometimes one is run by a single church, hospital, or other local organization. The goods they sell have been donated; their prices are excellent.

They generally do not have many pieces of furniture on hand, and many of them are small. Some operate central depots to which the goods are brought initially. These are listed in the telephone book, and if you want first crack at the furniture, this is where to go.

Chances are you will have to visit thrift shops many times before finding what you want, but their prices are very low and some of the pieces are excellent. You will find chairs and tables here for as little as five or ten dollars. Most of the stuff is well used, but on occasion you will find a really good piece.

Some Salvation Army depots and some others give every piece of wood furniture they receive a "pauper's coat" of red varnish. I do not know why they do it, and in most cases it does little to improve the piece.

The fact that local used-furniture dealers and antique dealers haunt these thrift shops is proof that they offer more than just junk. To beat these people to the punch you have to learn the collection schedules and get to the depot early, when the pickup truck comes in. This way you will also save the piece you may want from the coat of pauper red.

Most of the charity furniture centers handle a lot of furniture over the year, but it comes and goes quickly; you have to keep coming back to find what you want. If you are willing to make a few repairs, do some refinishing, and haul your own, they are well worth your investigation.

Garage sales. Also called tag sales, barn sales, and lawn sales, they have become very popular in America's suburbs. This is the way the Smiths dump the love seat they can't use and get the armchair they want and the Joneses can't use. You can never tell what you may find offered, and the prices are always good.

You can learn where a garage sale will be held by looking in your local shoppers' paper or for signs posted on poles, supermarket and church bulletin boards, etc.

Much that is offered is worthless, but some items may be highly usable. Matching pieces, sets, and the like are rare, but you will find coffee tables, ashtray stands, summer furniture, and one-of-a-kind items for sale. The prices are almost giveaway. Bargaining is normal, but the Smiths' garage is not a Middle Eastern bazaar; if the asking price is $10, don't start with a counter offer of $1 and expect to meet the seller halfway. And don't insult the sellers or their merchandise. You might try, "Would you consider an offer of X dollars?" But you may get slugged if you say, "You don't really expect to get $10 for this piece of junk, do you?"

Naturally, you haul your own, and all sales are final.

House wreckers, salvage yards. Companies that knock down old houses and other buildings sometimes have salvage yards where they sell the things they find. Usually these places have the big items: beds, dressers and even pianos, stained-glass windows, paneled doors, etc. Their prices vary, depending on the acumen of the operator and what the market will bear. You can bargain with these people, and you can also wait them out. If a piece does not sell, they will drop its price.

You will pay more here for furniture than at thrift shops, and the used furniture usually falls into the very-used-but-not-quite-antique category (except for an occasional antique they fail to spot).

Some advertise, some are listed in the phone book. Local lumberyards can direct you to them. Some have "Antiques For Sale" signs above their old shops and barns, but most of their antiques have not been sufficiently aged.

In all these places you are strictly on your own. When you are asked for more than a few dollars or offered an almost-antique, you had best be careful. Still, you can often pick up an attractive used piece here at a really good price, especially if you are prepared to do some touching up or refinishing.

Newspaper ads. With one family out of five now moving every year, there are a lot of people who would rather sell off some furniture than haul it across the country, and they use the classified ad to announce the sale. The ad may be in the regular local paper, or in the "shopper" papers that accept the ad at no cost and collect a percentage of the sale. You will often be able to pick up matching sets of furniture through these ads, along with rugs and wall hangings. Sometimes, if you make a sufficiently generous offer, the sellers will part with more items than they originally intended.

The serious sellers advertise in the commercial newspapers. Those who are not in a hurry to sell, or who are content to sit on an unrealistic price, more often advertise in the "shoppers."

Part of a large selection of used furniture on sale at a housewrecker's yard.

In any case, phone before you drive over. Always get a good description of the item and a firm price before investing your time in going to look at it. Have the courtesy to cancel a meeting if you find you cannot make it—discourtesy will always raise the selling price. And learn whether they will take your check before you go.

One more point: If you have no intention of paying the asking price, say so before you go. Sometimes the advertiser's ideas on pricing are more than a little strange. To go and then bargain is poor form. You might say, "If the furniture is what I can use and in like-new condition, as you say it is, I will pay what you ask, but if it is not, I hope you will not be insulted by an offer."

In the ads placed in the "free-ad" papers, you will find, on an average, less desirable furniture and accessories.

Both types of newspapers are excellent sources for bargain furniture, but do not expect to pick up what you want the first time you make a phone call, and don't give up just because the first few trips turn out to be a waste of time and gasoline.

"Furniture wanted" ads that you place yourself do not do nearly as well as "for sale" ads. People with the usual run of furniture to sell do not look in the paper for wanted ads. If you do place an ad of this type, take it at the week or longer rate; the chances of a single ad drawing the response you wish is mighty slim. Be specific, state your price, and don't chain yourself to the phone. A statement like "usually home after 6 P.M." will save you from having to sit by the telephone all day but won't limit the hours they may call too severely.

Scavenging. In our neighborhood it is customary for those who see something their neighbor has discarded and they can simply walk over and take it. This is considered sensible and economical and there is no onus attached. Scavenging in this fashion can get you used furniture at an unbeatable price.

The city dump is also a surprisingly good place to pick up useful pieces of furniture. You would be surprised by how many good pieces are discarded, and how many more things you'll find that can be converted to furniture, though not really meant to be furniture.

What can be done to make some of these things useful as furniture is discussed in Chapter 14.

WHOM CAN YOU TRUST?

There is one way of making reasonably certain you get a fair shake, and that is to deal with a long-established firm. The company may be large, it may be small. It may handle top-level merchandise, it may deal in low-priced furniture; no matter. If it has been in business a long time, it must be reasonably honest. The buying public does learn in time; after enough consumers have been burned, word gets around and the establishment goes defunct.

You can check out most companies at your local Better Business Bureau. You can also ask your friends and even ask the company itself for the names and addresses of some of their customers in your neighborhood. Reliable shops will give you this information.

But please, don't make the mistake of assuming that any shop that is willing to give you names is automatically non-suspect. Check the references.

MONEY IS NOT THE MEASURE

Is a $1500 couch one third better than a $1000 couch? Perhaps it is better, perhaps not. The dollar value of any item is determined by the price it brings. If a dealer can sell a couch for $1500, it is worth $1500, but only as measured in dollars. Remember that. The intrinsic value of the couch can be anything from zero on up. Will the more expensive couch or table be better made than the less expensive item? Perhaps, but not necessarily. Is an $18,000 Mercedes worth three $6,000 Fords? To some people, yes. To others no. Certainly the Mercedes is a little better made than the Ford; just as certainly it is not three times better made, nor will it last as long as three successive Fords.

Here is one example of how dollar-conscious consumers are often fooled. A furniture dealer receives two brand-new tables. They are identical, except one is veneered in teak, the other in walnut. Both cost the dealer an identical sum. According to the markup formula he uses (which is never less than double), he would normally put a price of $1,000 on each. But he is an experienced merchandiser. He marks one table $950, the other $1,150.

Some customers will select teak over walnut or vice versa because of taste. Others, who believe the more expensive table to be better will reason: If we are going to spend $950, why not go the extra money and get the best? Why not indeed if the more expensive item is truly so much better? But is it? This you can only determine by careful examination of the item after you have read this book and had some experience looking at furniture.

There is a median range for most items. There is a price range within which auto makers can produce satisfactory vehicles. When they go below this range, quality and rider comfort fall off rapidly. When they sell for much more, the price goes up very steeply in relation to the extras the purchaser receives.

It is the same with furniture. As you examine furniture offerings you will learn the current range of prices for reasonably satisfactory furniture. If you purchase furniture at prices much below this range through normal channels, you will receive comparatively little for your money. If you go much above this range, you will be paying a lot more for a little bit extra.

BEWARE THE RIP-OFF ADS

Rip-off ads show a piece of furniture in a beautiful setting, surrounded by unusually lovely wall hangings, plants, and other accessories. Very often the piece is made to look larger by putting it closer to the camera, or by accompanying it with under-sized accessories. Photographing children, instead of adults, on the couch gives an illusion of greater size.

The greatest rip-offs occur when a number of pieces are offered. The ad may read: "Seven-piece Living Room Set, only $777.00." The photograph shows a complete room, but the sideboard shown is not one of the seven pieces, and neither is the coffee table. The seven pieces includes a couch, two soft chairs, three cushions and a magazine rack—all in the photo. The ad is a come on. Once you have gone all the way to the furniture showroom you will be reluctant to leave. And even if you do not buy, your presence is valuable. The more people in a shop, the more the shop will sell. (How many times have you backed away from a restaurant because it was empty?)

Phony sales. The dealer advertises a table for $900. After a few weeks he holds a sale and offers the table for the unheard-of price of $450. This would be a bargain if the same table was not normally sold for the same price or even less. The fact there is a hefty price tag with a bold red line through it doesn't guarantee that the sale price is lower than usual.

OTHER SALES TRICKS

If you know that you are susceptible to sales pressure, buy in a department store on a charge account or pay by check. In this way, you have time for reflection. You can always stop the check or refuse to accept delivery. Once you pay cash, the burden of recovery is on you, and you better believe it; it is a burden. Here are some tricks that lure the unwary buyer:

Switch. This is a simple gimmick. An ad entices you into the shop with the promise of a tremendous bargain. When you arrive, the item is all sold out. (The ad *did* say "limited quantity.") Or, it turns out to be a piece of furniture you would not put in your dog's house.

Sometimes the advertised piece is very nice, really a bargain, but the salesperson steers you off. "I know all you young couples are a little short of cash.'' The salesperson looks around as though worried that someone is watching. ''The advertised table is $800. Now *this* table goes for $1,200, when it is in perfect condition. But it is not in perfect condition.'' He says this and scratches the table with a penknife. ''Now it is floor damaged. I can let you have it for $700.''

The salesperson has risked a good job for you nice people. And you nice people are in a sense party to the crime. What else can you do but buy?

Variations include switching sales tickets while the customer is watching; putting a sales ticket on furniture that is supposedly not on sale; selling a two-leaf dining room table in place of a single-leaf table, ''by mistake.'' In all these games the salesperson seems to be working against the company.

Don't believe any of this. You are being switched on company orders and the salesperson may even be getting an extra commission for making the switch. If the switch is supposedly dishonest, you are the victim of the dishonesty. The item you have been switched to is overpriced. In the case of the scratched table and other deliberately damaged goods, the item is then ''used,'' the seller is absolved of all responsibility and sells it in an as-is condition.

If you are merely being pushed to buy a better quality item, the effort is legitimate. Salespersons naturally want to sell as much as possible; in furniture sales they usually work partially on commission.

SETS, SUITES, AND GROUPS

Three different words for the same thing; two or more pieces of furniture based on a single design and color scheme and sold as a unit.

From the dealer's point of view, it is to his advantage to sell a set; it is at least two pieces in place of one. To aid his sale he will advance these arguments: The set will cost you less than the total price of the pieces purchased individually. The set will save you the trouble and problem of matching pieces. The set will insure that your pieces match, something that is chancey if you purchase one piece at a time over an extended period.

However, very often the set contains pieces you do not want or need. Why buy a table with more chairs than you will ever need? Constructed simultaneously, the parts of some sets are so patently identical as to be ridiculous and gauche. Or you may find one piece beautiful and the rest ugly. You may not want a roomful of exactly matched pieces. And the statement that the set sells for less than the sum of its parts is not necessarily true.

WHAT NOT TO BUY

Here is where the authors stick their necks out. One's taste should be one's own and not anyone else's. But we feel so strongly about the following that it would be unfair to leave our suggestions out of this guide.

Stay away from fads. A fad is temporary; that is what the word means. It is fun for only a short while, and if you cannot switch furniture as often as fads change, it is best not to start.

Stay away from blow-up furniture: the big balloons. They squeak, they lose air, and they are not comfortable.

Stay away from the pile-of-cushions furniture. The cushions slither around; they are not comfortable and they are far, far too expensive.

Stay away from slotted cardboard and papier mâché furniture. If you do not have sufficient funds to purchase anything better, make do with orange crates or thrift-shop items. Most of the paper furniture will not last the year, and it is a pity to waste your money when you have little.

Stay away from clear plastic furniture. Some of the modern acrylic designs are beautiful, but they will "frost" very quickly. The plastic is soft and is easily scratched and marred. A cigarette can melt a hole and leave a brown ring on its surface.

Stay away from gimmick furniture, the furniture that looks

like hands or lips or part of a boat. These are good for a chuckle, and if you have the wherewithal to replace your conversation pieces with each party, fine. But if you have to live with the stuff you will soon grow to hate it.

The same holds for overly ornate, overly large and overly bright furniture, rugs, and wall hangings. A blood red sofa may look good in a photograph, but facing it every day in the week can drive one bonkers.

Much of the stuff you see in the homemaking magazines has been assembled to produce startling color photographs. The rooms they have set up are impossible to live in. You will also find photos of designers' homes done this way to catch the public's eye.

If you cannot spend some time in a room you admire, don't copy it. It is one thing to examine a photograph of a room and quite another to sit in it for a day or so. And just because someone rich and famous has done their living room in a combination of apple green and black doesn't mean it is beautiful. Neither wealth nor fame is automatically accompanied by good taste and a sense of beauty.

Stay away from shag carpeting and rugs. The long pile on the shag merely hides the big open spaces between the piles. Shags show wear much more quickly and obviously than any other type of rug or carpet. If you cannot afford a standard weave, let it go until you can.

Stay away from expensive, printed reproductions of art works. For the same money or a little more you can purchase an original oil or watercolor, help a poor young artist and own an authentic original that may some day be valuable.

FINDING BARGAINS

How do you go about finding bargains in furniture? There are a number of ways. You can follow the ads and hope to recognize a bargain. You can haunt the thrift shops, auction rooms, and tag sales waiting for a real antique to go unrecognized by anyone but you. You can go to auctions, again hoping to see what no one else sees. You can wait for furniture sales; generally they go on after Christmas. You can visit showrooms and ask for floor samples or discontinued models. You can bargain with interior decorators. You can do business with individual furniture makers. You can buy used furniture and repair and refinish it. You can buy through the mails and even make your own furniture. There are many ways in which you can furnish your home beautifully at far lower cost than you can by just walking into the nearest shop and saying, "I want this and this." But it takes knowledge, time, and effort.

AVOIDING PROBLEMS

According to statistics, furniture buyers have more complaints than any other group of consumers. Their dissatisfactions range from scratched and damaged furniture to wrong and late deliveries—sometimes as late as six months. There is no way you can protect yourself against all of these possibilities, but here is how you can certainly reduce the chance of them happening to you.

Hold on to your options. Don't put down more than a small deposit on the purchase of any furniture. Pay the balance only as and when it is delivered. When delivered, have it all uncrated and inspect it all. If there are minor scratches, which are normal in this business, insist that the company refinisher show up and make the repair before you pay the entire bill. Do not send back slightly scratched furniture. It will only disappear for six months and then be delivered, possibly with new scratches.

If you are buying furniture from a department store on a charge account, ask that you not be billed more than a deposit until the furniture is delivered. If this is not possible, you can always hold up payment until delivery is made.

As we have said, don't buy furniture on time. If you do not have the money, think seriously about putting the purchase off. If you sign a time payment agreement with a furniture company or company, they discount the note (sell your debt) to a bank. You then owe the bank. No matter what your complaint may be, if you hold up payments to the bank, the bank will sue and ruin your credit elsewhere.

To force service or whatever from the vendor, you may have to sue. This is easy and inexpensive if the amount involved is under $1,000. Then you can hasten to the small claims court, and tell the judge directly. No lawyer is needed. If you have to engage a lawyer, think seriously about burning the furniture and moving into a tent. It may be less costly in the long run.

If you purchase furniture or anything else on a charge account you are again responsible for dealing with the vendor. Hold up charge account payments and you can be sued and have your credit ruined.

TREASURE THE HONEST DEALER

In this big, wide sea of dishonesty and deceit there are many islands of honesty and integrity. When you find an honest dealer, stick with him or her. Perhaps you will find they charge a few more dollars for their goods, but it is well worth it to know you are getting your money's worth.

Generally, these are merchants who do not offer world-beating bargains, who possibly have one or two clearance sales a year. They provide their own delivery, and have their own repairman on the staff. They do not *push*, and *they accept returns.*

They and their salespeople know furniture and will take the time to explain the differences and why one piece costs more than another. They do not stock faddish merchandise; they do not stock "garbage" or borax (junk), and they understand when you say you would like to look around before deciding.

How do you recognize them? Easy. You will sense their quality once you have entered their establishment and have spoken with them.

INTERIOR DESIGNERS

This is an area as wide open as any frontier town in the early West. Interior designers perform a specific function and naturally want to be paid. How they are paid and how much they are paid is difficult to pin down.

Store designers. Some furniture shops will tell their customers that every one of their salespeople is a trained designer and stands ready to assist the customer. This is nice, but it really means that if they aren't too busy they will tell you yes, this will go and this won't go with your room. As we said, this is nice.

Other stores will work from your floor sketch, with dimensions, position and widths of doorways, radiators, and windows. (With or without an interior designer, you should have this information on hand when you shop.) They have designers who will then spend some time with you and help you plan and select on the basis of your floor plan.

Still others will send a designer to your home when they are certain you plan to spend more than a certain minimum, or you have previously purchased a considerable quantity of furniture in their establishment.

To learn what design assistance you will be given and whether or not there is a charge or a minimum purchase requirement, ask the store manager. Do not ask a clerk, or you may, surprisingly, find yourself billed for the service.

Freelance designers. At this writing, in the New York City area, the going rate for freelance designer services is $250 plus a 10% finders fee on everything they buy for you. Since established designers can secure up to a 40% discount on much of the furniture they buy, they make money coming and going. One certain indication of the tremendous profit to be made in this profession is the intense competition that exists.

There is no reason why a designer purchasing a large number of expensive pieces cannot make money on the discount and still present you with a total bill lower than what you would pay if you bought directly. Perhaps some do, but we haven't met them.

Services rendered. Established designers are welcome in salons others cannot enter—a fact you will soon find out if you try to go to these places on your own. Experienced designers have a mind filled with data. We could spend weeks or even months looking for a specific antique, for example. There must be more than five hundred antique shops in New York's Manhattan alone. But a designer knows the shop most likely to carry what we want.

An experienced designer should know wood, furniture construction, fabrics, rugs, etc., and his or her services should be a guarantee that you won't end up with shoddy junk.

After discussion with the client, the designer selects the pieces that satisfy the client and the designer's own esthetic sense. The designer does the chasing, makes certain the correct pieces are received in satisfactory condition, helps position them, arranges the wall hangings, etc.

Now comes the moment of truth. Does the completed room live up to the picture you had when you discussed your ideas with the designer? Does it reflect your personality and lifestyle? Months may have passed between the discussion and the final setting up of the room; changes in your ideas may have taken place.

The best designer has a tremendous task in translating a client's mental image to physical reality. That is why designers always insist on a retainer before they start and that is why you must seriously ask yourself whether you will be happy with what someone else selects for you. Many of us are not.

It is difficult for the most sagacious and experienced interior designer to please your taste, your physical and emotional needs, and your pocketbook exactly. So if you do engage an interior designer, be fair. Don't ask for the world.

How do you find a good one? Ask your friends; ask the top-flight furniture dealers; check with the local Better Business Bureau, write to the American Society of Interior Designers, 730 Fifth Avenue, N.Y., N.Y. 10019, or the Interior Design Society, Merchandise Mart, Chicago, Ill. 60654.

DELIVERY

This is the sad part of our tale. Delivery of furniture is slow; very slow. The time lapse between signing a purchase order and actually seeing the furniture in your home can be anything up to several months. It all depends on the location of the manufacturer whose furniture you have purchased, whether a commercial carrier is delivering or the store's truck, and just how busy they may be.

If you are buying furniture that is on the showroom floor, and the company does its own deliveries, you may receive your goods that very afternoon. We do not advise you to bank on it. But it can happen.

Large establishments, chain stores, for example, often have commercial carriers deliver for them. This means your order must wait its turn with material purchased at hundreds of other shops by thousands of other people.

When the furniture is in the store's warehouse, the wait may not be too long.But when it is still at the factory, or worse yet, has to be manufactured—and you may not be told this— you'll have a long, long wait.

This is why you should never pay more than a deposit for any furniture until it is satisfactorily delivered. Otherwise you are in the position of not having any leverage on the seller. If you sign a time-payment sales contract, your payments continue to come due even though you may never have seen your furniture. Then your only recourse is to take the shop to court. If you refuse to pay the bank to whom you owe installment payments, they could take you to court and damage your credit rating.

A reliable house will tell you truly just how long a wait you should expect, even when it may discourage the sale. A reliable establishment will not insist upon full payment before delivery (except for a special, one-of-a kind order).

A shop may not be able to give you the exact day and hour of delivery. Very often, the best they can do is specify "some time on Tuesday; probably after noon." This is more common in the cities where parking is a problem and truckers cannot foretell how long each delivery will take.

16

Care and Cleaning

We have a rolltop desk in our office that has been in constant use for more than 100 years. It was made of oak by William Schwarzwaelder & Co. of New York in 1874. Its condition is not perfect, but it is very good. With a little care, this desk should be good for several more centuries of service.

A furniture lifetime such as this is not unusual. If the piece is well made to begin with, a little care should keep it alive and beautiful for generations and even centuries.

BASIC PRECAUTIONS

Use reasonable care. Don't tilt chairs, sit on their arms, or use an upholstered chair for a ladder. Don't sit on the edge of a bed. In less time than you might imagine, you will have a dent there. Mattresses are not designed to carry a concentrated load in any one place. (They would be too stiff.)

Tables are not repositories. Convenience often leads us to use polished wood end tables that are near a front door as a dumping place for keys, purses, and packages. In no time, the tabletop is covered with scratches, and you have the problem of refinishing the wood surface.

Always use trivets when placing hot dishes on a table. Finishes are very sensitive to temperature.

Watch the plates and dishes you put on a bare table. Chafing dishes, large platters, etc., sometimes have sharp edges on their bottoms. Inspect them all once in a while just to be certain all is well. Even if they are smooth, don't drag heavy dishes across a bare tabletop.

Keep all wood surfaces waxed. It doesn't matter if you use solid paste, wax in oil form, or spray. Wax two or three times a year for protection against dust. Without the wax coating, the dust becomes an abrasive when you wipe the furniture. In time this scouring action removes the gloss on the finish and sooner or later the finish itself. Wax also affords a slight protection against abrasion during ordinary use.

Wipe up all spills immediately—particularly alcohol and perfume (which contains alcohol). Alcohol will damage most furniture finishes.

Keep all unused upholstery covered. Slipcovers are most convenient, but if you do not have them, any all-covering piece of cloth will do. Uncovered upholstered furniture suffers damage from dust and light. (Even indirect sunlight is somewhat damaging.) You can never remove all the dust, and you cannot reverse fading at all.

Arm guards help. An arm guard is any piece of fabric placed on top of an upholstered arm or back to take up the wear at that point. Any attractive material can be used, and often leftover pieces of upholstery material are used. They are just trimmed and laid in place. Sometimes lead weights are sewn into their edges. When "real" company comes, they can be picked up and removed.

Coasters are a must on rugs. Protect your rugs or hardwood floors by placing coasters under all furniture legs except those of small chairs (not because they wouldn't be helpful there, too, but because the coasters are a nuisance when the chairs are used).

Deck the furniture with ashtrays. When you invite smokers into your home, have more than enough ashtrays.

Look behind the pillows. Check behind and beneath pillows every time you clean the room, and following every gathering. Sometimes you will find coins, which isn't bad, but sometimes you will find scraps of food, which could ruin the furniture if they are not quickly removed.

Vacuum the upholstery. When you do the rugs and carpets, use the attachment or hand vacuum and go over the upholstery lightly. DO NOT BEAT THE UPHOLSTERY. Doing so will damage the fabric more than it helps by cleaning it. (Don't beat rugs, either.)

Applying soil-proofing compounds. There are a number of these on the market. They come in spray cans, and are invisible when applied. The manufacturers claim that they keep upholstery from fading and soiling and make it waterproof. We wish we could assure you that any of them do exactly what is claimed. All we can do is strongly advise that you test a little on a sample of the upholstery material or on a hidden corner of the piece of furniture before you risk applying it to all the fabric.

Block the sunlight. Shield upholstery, rugs, tapestries, etc., from sunlight, which will bleach their colors. The reds and purples are most susceptible to the fading action of the sun.

Move your furniture about. Like the tires on an automobile, the various pieces of furniture in your home do not wear evenly. Some chairs and table corners receive more use than others. So, switch the pieces around every year or two. In this way you won't end up with one worn chair and five almost new ones.

Watch the moisture. An overly dry atmosphere, such as is common in most homes in winter, dries out furniture, particularly wicker and rattan, and loosens glue joints on other furniture. At the other extreme, a house whose interior is so moist that water condenses on walls and furniture leads to mildew and rot.

If your home is too dry, and you have hot air heat, add a moisturizer to your heating system. It will improve your health, save on your fuel bill (damp air is warmer than dry), and preserve your furniture. If you have hot water or steam heat, keep a kettle bubbling on very dry days.

Excessively moist interiors are generally brought about by

insufficient ventilation. This is common in homes that have metal or plastic siding on the exterior, and tight storm windows. Cover all cooking pots and keep a window open somewhere.

Damp cellars require special treatment. If you have just a little water in the cellar, it will probably be eliminated by the installation of one of the demoisturizers currently on the market. But inches of water on the cellar floor requires trenching and piping to drain the soil outside the building.

CLEANING TIPS
(See Chapter 10 for information on rug cleaning.)

Polishing requires care. Don't apply polish every time you dust the furniture. If you do you will soon cover the wood with a visible coat of wax. Use care to keep wax off upholstery fabric; it may stain the cloth permanently. Do not apply so much wax that you fill the grooves and indentations in ornamental carving.

Use a clean dust cloth. Soil is an abrasive, and a soiled dust cloth can cut through the wax and make tiny scratches in the finish, which after a while gives it a fogged look.

Vacuuming helps. Upholstered furniture should be lightly vacuumed every time you clean the room.

Wash spills on wood. If food is spilled on the wood portions of furniture, remove as much as you can with a damp cloth. Follow with a little soap and water and then dry with a clean cloth. Mild soap and lukewarm water will not harm furniture finish. Finally, rewax the area.

Attend to soils and stains immediately. Should someone spill food or drink on upholstery, do not wait until the party is over; clean it up immediately. To wait is to permit the soil to soak in and remain permanently.

Accumulated wax. You will know that you have too much wax and polish on your furniture when you cannot make it shine after waxing. To remove some of the wax, try polishing with a clean cloth. If that doesn't do it, pour a little alcohol on a clean rag and wipe off the wax. Do this quickly, taking care not to let any alcohol remain on the furniture. Any kind of alcohol will do; rubbing alcohol, painter's alcohol (wood alcohol)—even gin, but that's a waste if you are a drinking person.

Soil in crevices. Clean with a pointed stick or toothpick. Do not use a metal tool.

Insect infestation. Remove the offending furniture to a cleared space in the garage. Spray with the appropriate formula. The insect sprays available in the supermarket are fine. However, before you apply any spray, test it on a hidden corner of the fabric. Even if the spray does not adversely affect the fabric, do not soak the upholstery with spray fluid. This can easily damage it. Depend on repeated light sprayings rather than a downpour. For best results, cover the sprayed furniture with a plastic tarpaulin (sold in paint stores). *You must keep the plastic from contact with the furniture* since there is a good chance of an interaction between the plastic, the chemical spray, the fabric, and the finish on the wood that could stain the piece. (A few clean towels will keep the plastic clear of the furniture.)

SPOT AND STAIN REMOVAL TIPS

Work fast. As we've said, the more time that elapses between a spill and your attempt to clean it up, the greater the chance for staining.

A towel for liquids. Place the tip of a clean, dry towel gently against the edge of the spill. In some lucky instances the surface tension of the liquid will cause it to form a ball and remain on the surface of the upholstery, and you will be able, with care, to "lift" all the liquid and leave no residue. In any case, the more you lift, the less remains to soak into the fabric.

Never rub. Rubbing and muttering "out damned spot" is harmful. Rubbing breaks the surface tension of the liquid and enables it to enter the fabric more easily. The pressure of rubbing forces some of the liquid into the fabric, and the heat generated speeds staining, and that of course is exactly what you do not want. Rubbing also tends to spread the area covered by the spill.

Butter knife for goo and solids. Use a butter knife (or a palette knife if you have an artist in residence) and slide either tool gently beneath the blob. With care you can remove most of it.

Determine the nature of the spill. If the spill is oily, as butter, margarine or the like, you must treat it one way. If the spill is water soluble—soft drinks, whiskey or cocktails, etc.—you treat it another way. If you treat one like the other, you may make a far worse mess than if you had simply left it alone and gone about your business.

Oil spill. If the oily material is still soft, "pick it up" by applying an absorbent. Talcum powder, French chalk, cornmeal, and cornstarch are good absorbents. Fuller's earth, which can be purchased in many drugstores, is the best. Apply any of the absorbents by gently pouring them on the spot. Remove by gentle brushing and/or gentle vacuuming. If oil remains, apply more absorbent and remove it as many times as necessary.

Some commercial spot removers, such as Carbona's Spray Spot Remover, contain a solvent plus Fuller's earth. You can recognize the absorbent in these products by the white powder they deposit. Remove the powder after it dries by brushing or vacuuming gently.

Oily residue. You have removed as much of the oil spill as can be removed with repeated applications and removal of the absorbent. But some oil remains in the fabric. The best way to remove this residue is to wash it out with an oil solvent such as trichloroethane or perchloroethylene. You will find them in Carbona and other clear spot-removing compounds.

To wash out the oil spot, you must be able to get beneath the fabric and press a clean cloth under the spot. Then a little oil solvent is poured on the spot. When this has washed down and through, the cloth is moved a little to present a dry area beneath the spot. More solvent is dripped on the spot and so on until all the oil is gone.

If you cannot get under the oily spot, gently drip a little solvent on the spot, wait a moment and then touch the tip of a clean, dry white cloth to it. The dry cloth will "pick up"— absorb the solvent along with some oil. Repeat as many times as required, each time touching the spot with a fresh, dry and clean edge of the cloth.

Water-solvent spills. This category includes all water-soluble substances. Some spills will contain water plus an oil: ice cream, for example, and milk.

If the spill is mainly water, ginger ale, for example, pick it up by touching the tip of a dry, clean white cloth to the spot. When you can remove no more, wash through the spot if you can with water, or repeatedly drip water on the spot and dab at it with a dry clean cloth. Use the same procedures described for working with an oil solvent.

If water alone does no good, use one of the commercial combination solvents or cleaners such as Shout, Magic Pre-Wash, K2-B, or others. These contain soaps, oil solvents, and water. Again your best bet is to apply any of these and then wash them through the fabric. If you cannot do this, you must apply the solvent, add a little water and pick up, repeating the sequence as many times as necessary. But do not quit until all traces of both the spill and the cleaner have been removed.

Stains. In many unfortunate instances the spill will contain a color that will not disappear when the liquid and oils are removed. Now, you are in a different ball park altogether and there is a good chance you will lose the game.

What has happened is that the color in the spill or some chemical in it has reacted with the fabric to stain it; technically, the fabric has been dyed by the substances. Your possibly impossible mission is to remove the unwanted color without affecting the wanted color.

If you have tackled the spot with an oil solvent, try using one of the combination spot removers. If neither do any good, you have to try a bleach. The trick (and it is a good trick if you can do it) is to bleach out the stain without bleaching the fabric.

Bear in mind that bleach is time and temperature dependent. The longer it remains in place, the warmer the chemical, the faster it works and the more it accomplishes. So don't leave the bleach on the fabric and forget it. You may end up with a white spot.

Note too that all the bleaches can be diluted to reduce their strength and speed of action. And, that if the fabric is wet, not only will the action of the bleach be reduced, it will not leave a ring, or at least not so obvious a ring if things go wrong.

Bleaches to be used on natural fibers in order of increasing strengths:

White vinegar

Lemon juice

Hydrogen peroxide (medicinal peroxide)

Ammonia (good on food color stains)

Chlorine (standard household bleach)

Bleach for all synthetics

Clorox II, Snowy, etc. (dry powder bleaches; make a paste with water.)

CAUTION . . . CAUTION . . . CAUTION

Some upholstery fabrics can be damaged by oil solvents, combination solvents, soap or water. Be certain to test a hidden section of the fabric before going ahead.

Be careful with all bleaches. An unnoticed drop can leave a white spot behind. Pick up and wash clean, quickly.

17

Repairs

SURFACE DAMAGE, CLEAR-FINISH FURNITURE

Many very fine scratches. This is fairly common on old furniture and is called "checking" or "crazing." Clean the entire surface carefully with a clean dry cloth dipped in a little alcohol, use lukewarm water, a little detergent and a firm scrub brush. Follow with a clear water wash. Permit to dry thoroughly. Mix two parts turpentine, three parts varnish, and four parts boiled linseed oil. Apply with a pad of clean, dry cloth, using a circular motion. Do not apply more than a thin coating. Let dry hard. Repeat if necessary.

Small scratches. If the surface has been varnished, brush a little turpentine around the scratch or abrasion. The turpentine will dissolve the varnish, and it will flow into the crack.

If a lacquer has been used, apply a little lacquer thinner the same way.

If you do not know which finish has been used, try the turpentine first. It will not affect lacquer at all. Wait to make certain, then wipe the surface clean and try the thinner. Be careful, as splatters can leave marks.

Deep scratches. The standard method of repair consists of filling the scratch with stick shellac. These are literally small sticks of shellac; available in a number of shades at hardware shops and paint stores. If you cannot get an exact match you can mix two sticks by melting them and mixing them.

Clean the tip of a soldering iron. Touch the tip of the

shellac to the iron after it has heated up. Permit the shellac to drip into the crack until it is filled. If the tip of the iron is smooth, use it to smooth the shellac. If not, heat an artist's spatula on the iron or over an alcohol flame and use it to smooth the shellac. Finally, use #400 sandpaper on a flat board to make the surface of the patch flush with the rest of the wood.

SURFACE DAMAGE ON PAINTED FURNITURE

Burns, scratches. Smooth the area with fine sandpaper. Select spray-can paint to match. Apply to the bare area and beyond it for an inch or so. Permit to dry. Sandpaper with #400 sandpaper wrapped around a small, flat block of wood. Blow off the dust, spray, dry, and resand. Repeat until the damaged area is level with the balance of the wood surface.

Very deep scratches and gouges. Fill with wood putty. Permit to dry hard, sand and spray as many times as necessary, as described above. This cannot be used with clear-finished wood surfaces as the wood patch will be too obvious.

DENTS AND BLISTERS

Dents. Place a wet cloth on top of the dent. Apply a hot iron. The generated steam will often cause the compressed wood to expand. Be careful not to overheat and damage the rest of the wood surface. Repeat if necessary.

Blisters. Veneers sometimes blister. To correct, place a warm, wet cloth over the raised area. That will soften the veneer. Then, with a razor blade, slit the blister. With a small stick, alternately raise each side of the blister and force some wood glue underneath. Press the blister flat. Remove the excess glue. Place wax paper and a heavy weight on top until the glue dries.

LOOSE VENEER

Loose edges. Raise gently. Force wood glue underneath. Replace veneer and hold flat in place with clamps, weights or both. For a perfect job, veneer must be held perfectly flat and firmly against the wood.

Loose and raised central areas. Treat the same as suggested previously for a blister. Make certain to get glue all the way beneath the loose veneer. Make the slit with the grain of the veneer. Steam area first to soften veneer.

MISSING VENEER

The major problem is finding a new piece of veneer to match the existing piece. Veneers are sold by dealers in fine and rare woods. If your phone book doesn't list any dealers, ask at your lumber yard. As an alternative, haunt the city dump for old furniture that has matching veneer. Remove the finish from the surface of the veneer with paint remover. Follow with an alcohol wash. Then apply water until the glue loosens. To speed the process, cover the veneer with a wet towel, then apply a hot iron to the towel. When you have removed the veneer you need, let it dry before using.

Clean and cut the edges of the hole in the existing veneer. Align the grain of the patch with the existing veneer. Cut the patch to fit the hole. Use a sharp razor blade with a pressing, downward movement, rather than a cutting movement. Drawing the razor's edge across the veneer can sometimes cause it to split. Spread wood glue over the surface of the hole. Press the patch into place. Cover with wax paper and weights.

LOOSE LEGS

On tables. Look beneath the table for the bolt and nut that hold the leg in place. Tighten nut.

On chairs. Tighten wood screws that hold corner blocks and apron in place, if there are any. If all joints are glued, the best repair is to take the joint or joints apart. If you cannot force them without damaging the wood, place a hot wet towel over the joint. Place a tea kettle on a small electric stove beneath the chair. Position kettle spout beneath the towel. Bring water to a boil. That will soften the glue so that you will be able to pry the joint or joints apart. Remove all the old glue by sand-papering or with hot water. In the latter case, let the wood dry before applying more glue and reassembling the joint. Use carpenter clamps or make a clamp from rope to hold joint or joints together while the glue dries.

LOOSE WOOD JOINTS, GENERAL

If the glue block has come loose, drill holes through it, remove old glue, add fresh glue and replace. Install screws.

Other loose wood joints can be repaired as suggested previously.

DRAWER PROBLEMS

Drawer sticks. Empty the sticking drawer and the ones above and below it to make certain nothing in any of these is preventing proper closing. Try to close the drawer. See where it sticks. Plane down or sandpaper the spot.

If there are no high spots, rub candle wax on the runners; the wood itself may simply be a little rough.

Drawer too low. There is an unsightly gap between the top of the drawer and the enclosing cabinet. This is due to worn runners. Glue a thin strip of wood atop each runner. Wax surface of strip.

Drawer comes apart. Disassemble entire drawer. Remove old glue, add fresh glue and reassemble. Clamp parts together until glue hardens.

Loose knob. If tightening the screw doesn't help, remove the screw, slip a toothpick or sliver of wood into the screw hole, along with some glue. When the glue has set, reassemble.

WARPED TABLE LEAVES

Place on a support with weight in center to correct the

curve. Use sufficient weight to bend the leaf back beyond normal. (This process may take weeks.)

SUNKEN UPHOLSTERED SEATS

Turn over, replace torn webbing. Tighten and renail loose webbing. If individual springs are loose, tie them back down with heavy cord. Follow the system and spacing used in the piece originally. If tightening the webbing will not restore the seat bottom to its proper level, nail plywood slats 2 inches wide and ¼ inch thick beneath the webbing.

REPLACING PADDING COVERS

Remove the screws holding the seat and back pads in place. With a screwdriver remove the staples that hold the upholstery fabric in place. Cut and fit new upholstery fabric in place atop old padding. Staple new fabric to back of plywood, using ½-inch staples. (Staple guns can be rented.) Refasten the seat and back pads in place.

REPLACING CANED CHAIR SEATS AND BACKS

With a screwdriver (not a chisel) remove the spline. This is the narrow band of reed that circumscribes the old seating and holds the caning in place. If you have difficulty removing the spline, apply lukewarm water. You cannot reuse the spline, but keep a piece of it on hand as a purchasing guide. Next, remove all vestiges of the old cane from the groove the spline occupied. This groove must be made perfectly clean. If some of the cane adheres, apply warm water. This will soften the glue.

Buy a piece of machine cane big enough to extend 1 inch on all four sides of the spline groove. Buy a piece of spline with exactly the same cross section as the original. This must be long enough to fill the spline grooves.

Soak the new cane bottom in warm water for 20 minutes or so. Center the woven cane over the seat bottom. With a broad-tipped, pointed stick, drive the cane into the groove. Start at the center of one side. Drive an inch or two into place. Go to the opposite side of the seat. Drive another 1 or 2 inches into the groove. Now go to the center of either remaining side. Drive some more cane into the groove. Go to the center of the last side and do the same. Then work your way around the groove until all the cane has been driven into the groove. Doing this will pull the woven cane taut. Spread a bead of white wood glue along the bottom and sides of the entire groove. Now force the spline into the groove. Cut the end so that there is no overlap. Let the glue dry. Use a razor knife to trim the extra cane flush with the outside edges of the spline.

The same can be done with the back of the chair or any other caned surface.

To replace a cane chair seat, remove the old spline.

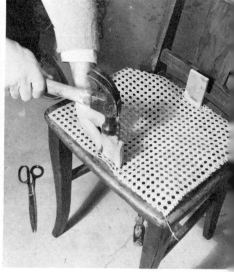

Use a piece of wood to drive new machine-woven cane into the spline groove.

If the caning has no spline but consists of strands of cane woven through a number of holes, you must reweave the seat bottom. Make careful note of how the original bottom has been woven, and purchase new cane in the identical width. Soak it to soften it. Then remove the old cane and reweave.

Prewoven or machine-made cane can be installed in a hour; hand weaving an area of equal size can take hours. You can purchase material for both, along with spline, at a crafts shop.

REWEAVING RUSH AND OTHER WOVEN SEATINGS

Some seat bottoms and backs are hand woven with reed, rush, sea grass, or similar material. If the weaving has been passed through holes, you will have to use material of equal or smaller diameter. If the material is wrapped around the chair or bench frame, you can use any material you wish.

If you are going to use cane, soak it in water for 20 minutes

Drive the new spline in place over the cane.

Reweave a worn chair seat with sea grass.

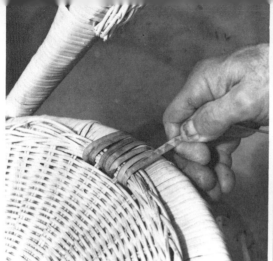

You can repair a woven chair seat with strips of cane if it is not too badly damaged.

or so before using to make it soft. If it stiffens as you work, wet it with a sponge.

Rush is a paper material. It should not be wet, as it will come apart. Work with it dry.

Sea grass is literally just that—sea-grass twisted into a kind of rope. It does not have to be softened. Since it comes in short lengths you will have to tie on a new piece frequently, or nail the ends to the inside of the chair.

Examine the weave of the original seat before you remove it, so you can copy it. Or, simply devise your own simple over-and-under pattern. The strength of the seating is not dependent on the weave pattern.

Except for cane, none of these seating materials need to be coated with anything. They are used as they are, but cane should be given a thin coating of clear varnish.

To fix broken sections of a reed chair, snip out the old reed and replace it with new, as in the illustration.

Glossary of Common Furniture Terms

ACACIA A tree similar to the locust, yielding a beautiful wood ranging in color from yellow brown to red and green. The Greeks used the leaf of this tree as the basis of their acanthus designs.

AMBULANTES Name for a small table designed to serve tea and which can easily be carried about. (French)

AMERICAN (furniture) Generally divided into: Early American; Federal, which started to appear after the Revolution; followed by Empire which imitated the French furniture of the time. This was followed by imitations of the styles of Europe up until roughly our Civil War, at which time Americans developed a more or less distinctive style of their own. Some of our 1860 to 1880 furniture is called Civil War furniture, and some of the pieces produced from 1880 to the start of the First World War is often styled Turn of the Century. The styles following this are usually grouped under Modern, with Art Deco as a subdivision.

ANGEL BED A bed with a partial canopy and narrow curtains at the sides. Chiefly French 18th century.

ANTIQUE Generally anything more than 100 years old.

ANTIQUING The process of treating furniture to make it look ancient. This may include anything from partially rubbed off coats of paint to blasts from a shotgun at twenty paces. Acid is also used to secure the desired appearance.

APPLE Wood from the tree on which apples grow; very hard, with a brown-pink color; excellent for carving and turning.

APPLIQUÉ Raised or cameo ornamentation, made separately and glued or nailed to the surface of the furniture.

ARKWRIGHT   Name of a family of early English cabinetmakers.

ARMOIRE   A tall box or cabinet of any kind with one or more vertical doors swinging outward, and standing free of any walls. Originally for arms, it is used chiefly today for clothes storage.

ARRAS   Tapestry used to drape bed and walls after the 4th century.

ART MODERN   French word for schools of American design during the 1920s.

ART NOUVEAU   Work of artists and craftspeople who, from 1875, departed from previously accepted styles.

ASH   A type of tree. Its wood is very dense, strong and light in color. Olive ash burls are beautifully figured and are often split into veneer.

ASPEN   A type of poplar. The wood is soft, light in weight and color. Used mainly in furniture as a veneer.

ASTRAGAL   Half-round molding, often used where doors meet.

AUBUSSON   Fine tapestries and rugs made in the French village with the same name.

BACK STOOL   An early chair without arms.

BAG TABLE   Small work or serving table with a bag fastened to one side and one or two drawers.

BAGUETTE   Molding that resembles a string of beads.

BAHUT   A small, rounded-top chest, held together with thin bands of iron and nails, originally used mainly for personal belongings. Some styles had leather coverings and were probably taken on trips, as luggage. Later, legs were added and it was used for kitchen and household goods. Still later, its legs were extended to make it a high cabinet.

BAKELITE   An early plastic still in use; generally black.

BALDACHIN   A number of columns supporting a canopy.

BALL-AND-CLAW   The end of a furniture leg carved to resemble a claw holding a ball.

BALL FOOT   The end of a leg turned to form a ball.

BALUSTER   A short, vertical column that supports a rail. Chair back pieces are also called this when they are long and vertical.

BAMBOO A rapidly growing grass that matures into hard, strong and flexible poles, internally separated by a solid section every foot or so. The external surface is golden yellow.

BANISTER BACK Chair backs composed solely of vertical members and a single cross piece at the top.

BAROQUE Excessive ornamentation, exaggerated shapes and design; started more or less at the start of the 17th century as a counter movement to what was considered the drab simplicity of earlier styles.

BARREL CHAIR A chair literally shaped like a barrel or even cut from one.

BASE The bottom piece of any furniture; the part that rests on the floor.

BASIN STAND A lightweight stand or table on which a wash basin sat. Sometimes made of thin metal.

BAS-RELIEF Carvings and sculptures that are part of the background from which they were cut and project from it only a very little.

BASSINET A small bed made expressly to hold an infant. Early bassinets were made of wicker and shaped like a long, shallow basket.

BASSWOOD A soft, light Amerian wood used mainly for low-cost furniture that is to be painted and for furniture carcasses that are to be veneered.

BATTEN Wood strips nailed or otherwise fastened across two or more boards.

BEARING RAILS Strips of wood that carry and guide a drawer.

BED BENCH A small, low bench placed at the foot of the bed.

BED BOLTS Bolts used to fasten bed rails to head and foot board portions of the bed.

BED RAILS The sides of a bed that carry and support the spring and mattress.

BED STEPS Steps made for climbing into high beds.

BENT WOOD Wood that has been steamed soft and then bent to a desired shape; furniture utilizing this process to some degree.

BEVEL A sloping, angled edge; also a chamfered edge.

BIDET   Small wash stand.

BIRCH   A family of trees. The white birches are soft; the red, black, and yellow are hard, take stain well, but are most frequently used for making cases.

BIRDSEYE   The small, circular figures seen when burls and other woods are cut through.

BLEACHED FINISH   A finish arrived at by bleaching the wood before it is varnished and/or stained.

BLOND WOOD FINISH   Light woods are left intact; some darker woods are bleached to secure light colors in finished work.

BOAT BED   A large, heavy bed shaped like a boat.

BOISERIE   French word for cabinetmaking.

BOMBE   A baroque style in which the front and sides (of chests, etc.) swell outward.

BONNETIERE   A tall, narrow and deep cabinet. (French)

BORAX   Early term for cheap, pretentious furniture. Today we might use the word "chintzy" in its place.

BORNE   A type of sofa, generally oval or round. (French)

BOSS   A raised ornament; a projection.

BOSTON ROCKER   An American rocking chair with an upward curving wood seat.

BOW BACK (FRONT, TOP)   Parts of furniture that curve upward and/or outward.

BOX BED   A box-shaped bed. Some have wood sides or curtains; some are folding.

BOX STOOL   A stool with a box top that could be used for storage of small objects.

BOXWOOD   Wood of trees belonging to the Buxus family; light yellow, heavy, hard, excellent for carving and turning.

BREAKFRONT   Furniture with a break or change in its forward surface. For example, a chest of drawers onto which is fastened a series of shelves. The front of the shelves is a distance farther back than the front of the chest.

BRIDAL CHEST A box for the collection of personal and other goods to be brought by the bride to her new home. Frequently made of or lined with cedar. Also called a dower chest or a hope chest.

BRITISH COLONIAL Furniture style developed by the British officials and settlers in the West Indies, South Africa, India, and other parts of the former British Empire.

BROCADE Cloth woven so that raised figures result. Originating in India, it is used for upholstery and drapery.

BROCATELLE Cloth, usually silk and usually having large woven patterns that appear to be embossed.

BRONZE An alloy made by mixing copper and tin. It is hard and fairly resistant to corrosion.

BUFFET A long, narrow table with or without one or more doors immediately below. It is positioned at the side of a dining room and used both as a food service table and for storage of linen and silverware.

BUILT-IN FURNITURE Any furniture constructed as an integral part of the house, either built-in when the house is built or later.

BULL'S-EYE MIRROR A circular, framed mirror, most often with a convex or concave glass.

BUREAU The word has seen a succession of meanings and usages. Today the term is most often used to describe a chest of drawers designed for use in a bedroom.

BURL When a tree trunk or limb is injured, the tree produces a roundish lump of wood, called a burl, at the point of injury. The grain within this lump or burl is complex and often filled with small dark spots called eyes. Burls are split into veneers and used for decorative purposes, because the wood in them is especially beautiful.

BUTTER CUPBOARD Ventilated cabinet used for food storage in early England.

BUTTERNUT A hard, beautiful wood often used for furniture. Has strong thorns 2 or more inches long.

BUTT JOINT One piece of wood joined directly to another.

BYZANTINE Pertaining to the period from about 476 to 1200 A.D., when what is now Turkey was occupied by the Romans, or to furniture in the style of that culture.

CABINET   A loose term for any upright piece of furniture with a vertical door. Lying down on its side, the same piece would be termed a box or chest.

CABINETMAKER   One who makes finely joined furniture of any kind.

CABRIOLE   Furniture legs that curve outward and then inward or have at least two curves going in different directions.

CAMEO   A small raised carving similar to bas-relief but smaller.

CANDLESTAND   A small, lightweight table made expressly for supporting candles.

CANE   Narrow strips of wood removed from the surface of rattan. Used in making seat bottoms, chair backs, etc. It is flexible, pale yellow, very hard on one side.

CAPITAL   The topmost portion of a pillar.

CARCASS   The body of a piece of furniture; often before it is veneered.

CARD TABLE   A small table made for playing card games. Its top is about 2 inches lower than a standard kitchen or dining room table.

CARLTON TABLE   Small table used for writing; English 18th and early 19th century.

CARTOUCHE   Complex, carved ornament usually including scrolls in the design, fastened to the surface of a piece of furniture.

CARYATIDS   Carved female figures that act as table legs, or in architecture, as building supports in place of or alongside columns.

CASE   A small container of any kind; also the frame or carcass—the body—of a piece of furniture before it is veneered or otherwise completed.

CASKET   Originally a small box or chest for storing valuables.

CASTERS   Small wheels or rollers attached to the legs of furniture, designed so that they will align themselves properly in any direction.

CHEST   A box or coffer with a hinged lid; the first piece of receptacle furniture made.

CHEST OF DRAWERS   A chest of any kind consisting of nothing but drawers that open horizontally on the chest's long side. May be on legs or rest directly on the floor. As a modern furniture term it is only used to describe chests that are several feet long.

CHIFFONIER   French term for a tall, narrow chest or bureau.

CHIMNEY FURNITURE   Andirons, coal scuttle, and all other fireplace accessories.

CHINA CLOSET OR CABINET   A cabinet with a glass front (and sometimes glass sides as well) intended primarily for the display of china.

CHINTZ   Low-priced cotton goods printed in bright colors and glazed.

CHIP CARVING   A wood carving technique where the chisel is used in short strokes.

CHIPPENDALE, THOMAS   The most famous of all English cabinetmakers (1718-1779). His name is often used to describe a style.

CIRCASSIAN WALNUT   One of the most beautiful of woods; complex figuring, with dark stripes on a light yellow background. The tree is found in southeastern Europe.

CLASSIC   A term used to describe furniture styled after ancient Greek and Roman designs.

CLAVICHORD   A percussion instrument with strings much like the modern piano, which followed it.

CLAW AND BALL   End of leg carved to resemble an animal claw clutching a ball.

CLEAT   A strip of wood fastened across two or more boards to hold them together or support something else.

COASTER   An early name for today's tea wagons or serving carts. Originally the English made them from trays with casters; some were shaped like barrels.

COFFEE TABLE   Any low table designed to stand in front of a sofa, couch, or settee. The table's top is usually lower than the seats of this furniture.

COFFER   A type of chest, usually of a size that permitted it to also be used as a seat.

COIN   Old English term for a cupboard that fitted into a corner.

COLONIAL   Designs, styles, and materials characteristic of America before 1776.

COLUMN   A vertical member of a piece of furniture or structure. It is generally massive in relation to the other parts.

COMB BACK   A chair with a second back higher than and behind the first. A Windsor chair design.

COMMODE   Either a chest or cabinet with doors and very short legs that is used for storage, or structures used by our forefathers to hide chamber pots.

CORNER CUPBOARD   A cupboard designed to fit into a corner; generally for the storage and display of china.

COUCH   Today, used interchangeably with "sofa." Previously used to define a sofa that had a back but no arms.

COX, JOSEPH   An 18th-century cabinetmaker and upholsterer from New York City.

CREDENZA   A side table or sideboard in heavy Gothic style.

CRICKET   A three-legged English milking stool.

CROSS STRETCHER   The lengths of wood that stretch from one chair leg diagonally to an opposite leg to brace the chair.

CUPBOARD   Any box or cabinet with doors at the front, used for storage. Receptacles that open at the top are chests.

CYPRESS   A tree with dark red wood that grows in swamps; the wood is fairly hard and greatly resistant to rot.

DAIS   A raised platform.

DAMASK   A very fine silk fabric used for draperies and upholstery. Its name comes from "Damascus," where it was first made in the 12th century.

DAVENPORT   A sofa (originally a small writing desk).

DAYBED   A chaise longue or similar piece of furniture on which an individual may rest without troubling to spread sheets, etc. The term is used for any number of designs fulfilling this basic application.

DEAL   Name used in England for pine, particularly Scotch pine.

DESK Originally a desk box; now any table or similar structure used for writing. Covered with a cloth by the French, the desk became bureau after *bure*, the French word for woolen cloth.

DESK BOX A small flat box containing a writing surface and writing equipment. The precursor of the attaché case.

DIRECTOIRE The period from approximately 1799 to 1804 in France, when classic Greek and Roman motifs were introduced into furniture.

DIVAN (See Sofa.)

DOUBLE CHEST Two chests of drawers, the upper portion somewhat smaller than the lower; generally constructed as a unit.

DOWER CHEST (See Bridal Chest.)

DRAPERY Any cloth hung over walls and windows for decoration. Originally used as a means of retaining heat.

DRESSER A chest of drawers topped by a mirror.

DRESSING MIRROR A small, self-supporting mirror.

DRESSING TABLE Any table equipped with drawers and a mirror, and having a place for one's legs, so the user can sit close to the mirror.

DRESSOIR A form of credenza having a serving surface used as a sideboard and a number of open shelves above for china storage.

DROP FRONT A door hinged horizontally so that it can be "dropped" forward to provide a horizontal surface.

DROP LEAF TABLE A table with a hinged leaf or leaves that can be folded down.

DRUM TABLE Small table having a round top and somewhat resembling a drum.

DUMB WAITER (British) A small stand with several circular trays above one another on a central post. The trays revolve and are used for serving food.

DUTCH COLONIAL Styles developed when the Dutch governed colonies in the New World. Furniture made during this period used wood native to the northeastern United States.

EASY CHAIR   Any large upholstered chair constructed mainly for comfort.

EBÉNISTE   Cabinetmakers in France who specialized in working with ebony.

EBONY   A very hard, usually black wood, prized for its color and the beautiful way in which it takes polishing. The blackest comes from the Gaboon in Africa. Ebony from Macassar is striped with light orange and deep brown.

ELIZABETHAN   Styles and designs developed and popularized during the reign of Elizabeth I of England.

ELM   A generally light brown wood similar in texture to oak, but not as strong. Today it is used mainly for veneer; it is too scarce for solid work.

EMPIRE   Styles and designs in fashion during the first French Empire (1804-1815). The furniture was large and heavy, with ornate carving, etc. Many motifs were inspired by ancient Egypt.

ENAMEL   A paint containing a high percentage of varnish or similar material. Dries slowly and has a high shine.

ESCUTCHEON   Originally a coat of arms, crest or monogram. Today, a worked plate of metal used to finish off or protect an area, as for example over a keyhole.

FAÇADE   The front of a building or of a piece of furniture.

FACING   Another term for applying a veneer, or for the veneer itself.

FARTHINGALE CHAIR   A straight-backed chair, usually upholstered and without arms, popular during the reigns of Elizabeth I and James I in England.

FAUTEUIL   A french version of the Farthingale chair.

FEDERAL   Furniture of the American Federal period—1780 to 1830.

FIDDLEBACK   Chair having a splayed back somewhat resembling part of a violin. Also a type of veneering that results in a series of opposing curls in the figuring.

FIGURE   The pattern and color of the grain in various woods. It is emphasized by cutting the wood into boards and particularly into veneers.

FINISH   The last step in the construction of furniture. Generally it consists of applying a layer of some sealing and protective agent, which typically may be wax, oil paint, or varnish.

FIR   Any of a group of trees of the pine family. Their wood is rarely used for furniture except for parts of carcasses.

FITTINGS   Term given to metal parts attached to furniture; handles, knobs, leg ends, etc. Also called hardware.

FLIP-TOP TABLE   A small table that folds and unfolds like a book.

FLUTES, FLUTING   Vertical grooves and channels cut into furniture for decorative purposes.

FOLIO STAND   A stand designed to hold a book for a reader who is standing.

FOURPOSTER, FOURPOSTER BED   Any bed with elongated corner posts, with or without a canopy overhead.

FRAME   Any wooden structure that surrounds or supports other parts, as for example a picture or mirror frame, a bed frame, chair frame.

FRUITWOOD   The wood of any fruit tree.

FUNCTIONALISM   A principle of design that holds that an object's function should determine its appearance.

GAME TABLE   Any of a number of small tables designed specifically for playing games.

GATELEG TABLE   Any table with drop leaves supported by legs that swing to or fold back so the leaves can be shut down for storage.

GEORGIAN   Furniture developed during the years 1714 to 1795 when the three Georges ruled England.

GESSO   A mixture of powdered stone and glue molded into various shapes and used to embellish furniture. Its purpose is to replace expensive hand carving.

GLAZING   In furniture finishing, to cover a surface with a thin coat of paint and follow with a clear coat of lacquer or varnish. The method simulates age, and changes the color and appearance of the wood.

GOBELIN   French tapestry makers from 1429. The French government purchased their factory in 1662 and made upholstery. In the 18th century Gobelin began again to make tapestries and in 1826 the company began also to produce carpets.

GONDOLA   Sofas and chairs with arms and backs that form one continuous curve.

GOTHIC   Furniture made in the Gothic period 1100 to 1500 and resembling Gothic churches in either overall design or ornamentation.

GOUGE CARVING   A simple, sometimes crude method of carving using a gouge, a chisel with a curved blade.

GRAIN   The fibers of wood.

GRAINING   A paint process that simulates the appearance of grain on an otherwise uninteresting flat wood surface.

GRANDFATHER'S CHAIR   A large armchair, generally upholstered.

GRANDFATHER'S CLOCK   A pendulum clock with a case tall enough to stand upright on the floor.

GRECO-ROMAN   The styles characteristic of Greek-influenced Rome in the years from approximately 200 B.C. to 200 A.D.

GREEK, ANCIENT   Generally refers to the so-called Golden Age of Greece, 1200 to 300 B.C.

GRIFFIN   Also called a Gryphone, a grotesque beast, half eagle half lion, carved in full form and in bas-relief as a decoration.

GRILL   A type of lattice or a pierced sheet usually of metal, rarely of wood. Used in bookcases, cabinets, doors, etc., either as a support for glass or in place of it.

GROS POINT   A coarse stitch devised by the French and used to embroider upholstery materials for furniture.

GUMWOOD   A strong, moderately hard wood that takes stain well, but must be carefully fastened to prevent warping. Three species are used: sweet, tupelo, and black gum. Often disguised as mahogany or walnut.

HALF TURNING   A turned piece that is later split in half, and each half then fastened to the side of a piece of furniture.

HALL CLOCK   Another name for a grandfather's clock.

HALL TREE   Also called clothes tree, used for hanging coats, etc.

HANGINGS   Portable wall coverings, such as curtains.

HARDWARE   Any metal part used to join or decorate furniture with the exception of nails and screws.

HASP   A kind of hinge that accepts a padlock.

HASSOCK   A completely upholstered footstool or one covered so that its wood frame is not visible.

HEPPLEWHITE, GEORGE   Famous English furniture maker of the 18th century.

HICKORY   One of the toughest, strongest of the American woods. It has the color of oak and bends well, but is difficult to work because of its hardness.

HIGHBOY   A tall, two-section chest of drawers, with the upper section considerably shallower than the lower so that the top of the lower section forms a table surface.

HIGH RELIEF   Relief carving that is very deep so that the figures stand out sharply.

HITCHCOCK   An American chair design of the 1820-1850 period, named after Lambert Hitchcock of Connecticut.

HOPE CHEST   An alternate name for dower chest.

HOUSING   The piece of wood that encloses a second piece in a wooden joint.

H-STRETCHER   The center crosspiece joining two stretchers. (Chair leg braces.)

HUTCH   A cabinet with doors supported on moderately tall legs. The name derives from the French *Huche*. Also an open shelf cabinet atop a chest of drawers or a swing-door cabinet.

IMBRICATION   Wood carving that has a pattern like fish scales.

INLAY   Wood decorated with inset pieces of other materials, such as other woods.

INTAGLIO   Carving in reverse. The design is cut into the surface, making the background of the design raised.

IRISH CHIPPENDALE   Mahogany furniture purportedly made in Ireland sometime after 1750 after Chippendale's published designs.

JACOBEAN   A term loosely applied to English furniture prior to 1688, derived from the Latin name for King James of England, Jacobus.

JAPANNING   The Far Eastern technique of drying successive coats of enamel under heat. The result is a very hard, shiny, and durable finish.

JIG SAW   A fine-bladed saw that can be used to cut small arcs and other curved shapes. Often used to do pierced work and lattice work.

JOINERY   The art or craft of joining pieces of wood by fitting one piece into another.

KERF   A saw cut or a series of saw cuts on the inner side of a board to facilitate bending it.

KIDNEY TABLE   Table or bench whose top is shaped like the human kidney.

KNOCKED DOWN   Furniture delivered disassembled and designed to be assembled easily. Also called ''KC.''

KNOTTY PINE   Pine wood with knots. The knots are very hard and run transverse to the board. The knot-free wood, which is called ''clear,'' is soft. The knots remain high when the rest of the wood wears down.

LABURNUM   Known as Corsican ebony in ancient Rome, the wood of laburnum is a hardwood, yellow in color and streaked with brown. It polishes to a high gloss and was much favored for veneer.

LACQUER   A modern quick-drying furniture finish. It can be clear, tinted, or opaque. Lacquer dries hard and can be rubbed to a high gloss or a satin finish.

LADDERBACK CHAIR   Chair with a series of horizontal slats across its back. The Pilgrims fancied these.

LANNUIER, CHARLES HONORE   A cabinetmaker from France who worked in New York City at the time of Duncan Phyfe. Some of Lannuier's work is falsely ascribed to Phyfe.

LATHE A machine that rotates the material being cut to produce round shapes like spools, urns, etc.

LATTICE Any flat or decorated surface pierced by a large number of holes to form a design that passes air and light.

LAZY SUSAN One or more circular trays that rotate on their common center.

LECTUS An ancient Roman bed.

LIGNUM VITAE Especially hard and dense wood from the West Indies.

LIME WHITENING A 16th-century technique for bleaching furniture by the application of lime (calcium oxide).

LIT-CLOS French terms for an enclosure, fixed or movable, that surrounds a bed.

LIVERY CUPBOARD A cupboard with pierced doors used for storing food in the bedroom so that occupants would not have far to go should hunger strike before morning. Also used in early English kitchens for food storage.

MAHOGANY A tree with medium hard wood with a reddish brown color, greatly prized for making furniture. Used so much during the 1700s that this century is called "the age of mahogany." The wood grows in many countries and there are a number of varieties. The color depends upon species and finishing.

MAPLE Found mainly in America, maple is a very hard wood, light in color and having extensive and complicated figuring according to the specific species and the portion of the tree from which it is cut. Used solid and as veneer. Though hard and tough, this wood rots quickly when exposed to weather.

MARBLE A form of limestone. The most beautiful (and expensive) is the green variety.

MARBLING A painting technique that produces the appearance of marble on wood.

MARQUETRY Flush inlay of woods and other materials of contrasting colors and figuring to produce a design.

MECHANICAL FURNITURE A general term for any furniture

that folds or incorporates a mechanism: swivel chairs, couches that convert to beds, etc.

MEDALLION   A carved and relatively flat-, round-, square-, or oval-shaped ornament fastened on a surface.

MENUISIER   French term for carpenter, joiner or cabinetmaker.

MEUBLES   French term for furniture that is easily moved or designed to be moved

MISSION   A style of furniture purportedly developed in the Spanish missions of our Southwest. Heavy, dark, with crude, visible joinery to imply rustic simplicity.

MITER   A joint where two pieces or wood are joined at an angle.

MODERN FURNITURE   Designs developed after World War I (1918). Some have flowing lines and graceful curves, but without the excess of older styles.

MOHAIR   A fabric made from the hair of the angora goat.

MOLDING   In woodwork, a long piece of wood shaped to a curve or combination of curves and angles along one, two, or three sides. In art, shaping a material by pressure as contrasted to shaping by filing, cutting, and chiseling. Clay may be molded; marble cannot.

MORRIS CHAIR   A type of easy chair with an adjustable back, invented by William Morris in the late 19th century.

MORTISE   A common woodwork joint consisting of one member with a hole, and a second member with a projection shaped to fit neatly into it.

MOSAIC   A picture or design constructed by embedding small pieces of colored material into a solid-color base.

MOSS   A plant used as upholstery stuffing in cheap furniture.

MOTHER-OF-PEARL   The inside lining of oyster shells used for inlay and similar work.

MOTIF   The basic design or approach of a piece of furniture. For example the major motif of the Gothic period was the suggestion of a church.

MUDEJAR   A combined Moorish/Spanish style limited to the period 1250 to 1500 in Spain.

MULLION   The vertical bars of wood or metal that divide a window into two or more panes of glass.

MUNTIN   The inside vertical portions of a window or door frame.

MYRTLE   A tree from our Pacific Coast whose wood is used in fine furniture. It is light tan in color, with a beautiful grain. Used mostly for veneering and inlay.

NEEDLEWORK   Upholstery made by embroidering canvas with woolen threads.

NEOCLASSIC   New furniture designs that lean heavily on the designs of the classic period.

NEO-GREEK   New furniture that draws on classic Greek furniture for its design inspiration.

NEST OF DRAWERS   A number of small drawers within a very much larger piece of furniture or their own small cabinet or case.

NEST OF TABLES   A number of tables shaped and sized to be fitted one beneath or within another.

NEWPORT SCHOOL   A group of Rhode Island cabinetmakers of the mid-1700s.

NORMAN   The furniture and styles of the French who conquered England in 1066.

OAK   A tree with hard, strong durable wood with coarse grain. Various species are found in most of the temperate zones of the world. Most of the wood is pale yellow to pale red.

OCCASIONAL TABLE   Any small table for serving coffee, displaying books, etc.

OGEE   An arch shape having a point at its top.

OGIVE   Sometimes "ogical"—having an ogee shape, or Gothic in style.

OLIVE WOOD   A greenish-yellow, very hard and close-grained wood much prized since ancient times for furniture. Now because of its scarcity its use is limited mainly to inlay and veneer.

ORIENTAL   In furniture, the styles developed by or derived from the Near East as well as China and other Eastern countries.

ORIENTAL WALNUT   Sometimes called Queensland walnut, this is a hardwood tree of the laurel family that grows in Australaia.

ORMOLU   A French term for metal ornaments more complex than a medallion or escutcheon applied to the surface of furniture.

OTTOMAN   A heavily upholstered seat or bench without a back, named after the Ottoman Turks of the early 1700s.

OVERLAY   Veneer applied to the surface of the wood.

OVERSTUFFED FURNITURE   Heavily upholstered furniture with no portion of the wood frame visible.

OYSTERING   Veneers made by cutting across a small branch to produce circular and oval pieces, which are then used as inlays.

PAINTED FURNITURE   In furniture, two meanings: First, the furniture is given a single or a number of coats of solid colors. Second, having decorations of simple flowers, leaves, etc., or actual, careful detailed oil paintings in contrast to the base, which may be varnished or painted. In some cases a thick layer of paint is permitted to harden on the surface, forming a type of cameo or bas-relief effect.

PANEL   A board held in place by parts of the furniture.

PAPIER-MÂCHÉ   Paper that has been soaked in liquid glue and molded into shape. When dry, it may be varnished and/or painted. Once used for furniture; still used for bowls, trays, tabletops, and the like.

PATINA   The change in surface texture and color produced by exposure to weather or air over a long time. Copper, for example, develops a green patina when it weathers.

PEARWOOD   A very hard, close-grained wood excellent for furniture and inlay. Much used in European provincial furniture.

PEDESTAL DESK   Another term for a knee hole desk, though some designs have a bank of drawers on one side only. The top is flat.

PEDESTAL TABLE   Any table with a top supported by a single central leg or column; usually round or oval.

PEDIMENT   In furniture and architecture, the ornament that is positioned at the top of the piece, or over a doorway. Generally it consists of two or more curves.

PEMBROKE TABLE A small table with a square, rectangular or oval shape when open and having two portions of the top on hinges—drop leaves—so that they can be lowered. Generally with a small drawer at one end.

PENDANT Any type of hanging ornament, also called a drop.

PENNSYLVANIA DUTCH The furniture design characteristic of the German and Swiss peoples who settled in eastern Pennsylvania. It is a simplified style frequently decorated with paintings of flowers and other earthy figures.

PERIOD FURNITURE Any furniture with a design so distinctive it can be traced to one of the famous period of furniture making; or a piece actually constructed during that period.

PHILADELPHIA CHIPPENDALE Furniture based on Chippendale styles and construction method and made in the mid-1700s by a group of cabinetmakers in Philadelphia.

PHILIPPINE MAHOGANY A comparatively soft wood, grown in the Philippines and unrelated to true mahogany except in color. Widely used for the surface veneer of plywood panels. It is actually *luan*.

PHYFE, DUNCAN Perhaps the most distinguished of the American cabinetmakers of the late 18th and early 19th centuries. Born in Scotland, he began working in Albany and then moved to New York City, where he operated a factory. He died in 1854.

PICKLED FINISH The wood is literally pickled (soaked) in any of various solutions to produce a white patina, in imitation of the patina on early English pine furniture. This was achieved by coating the furniture with plaster to make it smooth, and then removing the plaster with vinegar.

PIERCED CARVINGS Any carving with holes or piercings extending through the wood or stone.

PIETRA DURA Pieces of marble and other stones embedded in cement and then ground to a flat, smooth surface and used for a tabletop, etc. Today it is often called terrazzo.

PINE Various types of evergreen trees; their wood is very soft with hard resinous knots. Last choice for furniture making. Clear pine, which is simply portions of the tree without many knots, is used for moldings and some carving.

PLINTH   The lowest part of a column or pedestal; that upon which it rests.

PLYWOOD   Wood that is slit into thin sheets which then are glued to one another with their grain at alternate angles. In this way the tendency of one sheet of wood to split in one direction is offset by another sheet with its grain counter to the first. It is stronger than any single piece of wood, and its appearance depends on the topmost sheet of veneer, which can be of any wood or even many pieces of veneer joined in marquetry.

There are many grades of plywood. Some will come apart as soon as they are soaked. Others will withstand immersion for years and are used for constructing boats and even airplanes.

POLYCHROME   A grouping of many colors.

POPLAR   Trees with soft, pale lightweight wood used for the cores of plywood and for furniture carcasses.

PRIMAVERA   A white-colored mahogany.

PROVINCIAL   Styles developed in the provinces, away from the capitals of the country and therefore lacking the sophistication and more often the excesses of urban furniture.

PURITAN   Very simple, functional furniture devised by the Puritans of 17th-century New England.

QUARTERED   Flat boards are sawed from logs cut into four quarters lengthwise. The boards have the grain running the short distance through the thickness of the board, rather than its width. Quartered boards are less likely to warp and blister.

QUEEN ANNE   Furniture developed during the reign of the English Queen, 1702 to 1714. It is a very soft, graceful style based to some extent on the Netherlands-Baroque furniture imported by William of Orange.

RAILS   Any horizontal member or part of a piece of furniture that holds something, as for example a wood panel, or the spring of a bed.

RATTAN   A species of palm tree native to the Far Eastern tropics. It grows vinelike to lengths of as much as 500 feet. Diameter varies from 3/8 inch to several inches. When thorny bark and leaves are removed, the uncovered light-yellow wood is used for rope, furniture, and similar applications.

READING STAND A small table with a top that can be adjusted to support a book or sheet music.

RECAMIER A chaise longue with both sides and ends raised at a slight angle. One end is often higher than the other.

RECESS CABINET A cabinet designed to fit into a recess in a wall.

REDWOOD Also known as sequoia. The wood is red-brown in color. Too soft for indoor furniture, but excellent for furniture with thick sections that is to be used outdoors, as it resists rot and most insects.

REFECTORY TABLE A long, comparatively narrow table like those in the refectories where monks of the Middle Ages and later took their meals.

REGENCE That period in France following the end of the reign of Louis XIV until Louis XV ascended the throne: the years 1715 to 1725.

REGENCY In England, the period when George, Prince of Wales, was Regent beginning approximately in 1793 and ending in 1820.

RELIEF Differs from bas-relief in that the figure or sculpture is raised higher from the supporting base.

RENAISSANCE Awakening or rebirth: the period following the Dark Ages in Europe when interest in the culture of ancient Rome and Greece was renewed. The 14th to the 16th century.

REPLICA An accurate copy of an old or ancient piece of furniture, utilizing the same wood, construction technique, etc.

REPRODUCTION Copies of old pieces of furniture not as carefully made as a replica and generally produced using modern methods and techniques.

REST BED An old term for a chaise longue, day bed, or couch; any bed on which one normally does not sleep the night through.

RESTORATION (Period) In England, from 1660 to 1688. In France, from 1814 through 1830, less the Hundred Days when Napoleon returned to power.

RESTORATION (technique) The term used to denote the restoring of antique furniture to display or useful condition. When the term is applied loosely it may mean that nothing more than a chair's leg, for example, is original; the rest may be new.

ROCOCO Eighteenth-century European art and crafts character-ized by an excessive amount of ornamentation, in contrast to the more subdued ornamentation of the classical styles.

ROLLTOP A type of desk with a cover that rolls down to hide the writing surface and possibly nest of drawers. The movable top may be solid or composed of slats held together by canvas.

ROMANESQUE A European style dating roughly from 500 to 1100 A.D. that followed the Roman style but did not copy it.

ROSEWOOD Several species of tropical woods fall into this classifi-cation. When freshly cut rosewood exudes the odor of roses. The wood is very hard, dense, red-brown in color and takes polish very well because of its resin. Sometimes called tulipwood in England and America, its origin is India and Brazil.

ROTTENSTONE A very soft stone used for polishing.

ROUNDEL Any ornamental disk. Common term for handblown glass disks used in making stained glass windows, etc.

RUNNER Strip of wood beneath a drawer that helps hold the drawer steady; the curved lower stretchers that carry the legs of a rocking chair.

RUSTIC FURNITURE Any furniture crudely made because no bet-ter materials and skills are available, or to resemble these genuinely crude pieces.

SADDLE CHAIR Chair constructed to somewhat resemble a saddle.

SARACENIC Saracen influence that reached into Europe through Spain from about 700 A.D. and after.

SATINWOOD Hard, fine-grained wood from Ceylon, India, and the West Indies; light-honey colored.

SAVERY, WILLIAM Cabinetmaker of Philadelphia, 1721 to 1787. He produced a highly ornamented Chippendale style.

SCISSORS CHAIR A folding chair first made in ancient Egypt.

SCROLL In furniture a spiral or convoluted ornament or ornamen-tation, as a scroll-carved table leg.

SECRETARY Also Secrétaire, a cabinet with one or more drawers mounted on legs and having a fall front—a wide board that can be lowered from a vertical to a horizontal position to provide a writing surface. In Europe a secretary is sometimes called a bureau.

SECTIONAL FURNITURE Furniture made in sections or units that can be used together or stand alone.

SERPENTINE A form of surface or ornamentation with a snake-like, weaving, undulating effect.

SETTEE A bench with a back and low or no arms. Sometimes upholstered and decorated.

SETTLE A kind of settee usually permanently fastened to the floor and often with hinged seat covering a storage box. Rarely upholstered.

SÈVRES Objects made of porcelain in Sèvres, France, from 1756 onward. Some were used as furniture decorations.

SHAKER In furniture, the simple style developed by the American Shakers from 1850 onward.

SHAPED WORK Wood surfaces that are curved in some way other than carved.

SHELF CLOCK Literally small clocks of wood, metal, or porcelain designed to be placed on a shelf.

SHELLAC A secretion of the lac insect dissolved in alcohol, an ancient wood finishing and sealing agent. Often used on floors and under varnish on furniture. Cannot be used alone on furniture as it softens when warm.

SHERATON, THOMAS An 18th-century English cabinetmaker. His book *The Cabinetmaker And Upholsterer's Book* (1790) and others he published influenced cabinetmakers of his time. While he reproduced extant styles, these styles became credited to him.

SHIELD BACK A chair back shaped to look somewhat like a shield.

SHOJI A screen panel from Japan.

SHOW WOOD The easily visible wood on a piece of furniture.

SHOWCASE Any cabinet with one or more glass windows displaying the objects within.

SIAMOISE   A love seat with an S-shape so that occupants face in opposite directions.

SIDE CHAIR   A small chair without arms.

SIDE RAILS   The long narrow, on-edge boards that connect head-boards and footboards of beds.

SIDE TABLES   Tables that are placed alongside a wall, the end of a sofa or an armchair.

SIDEBOARD BUFFET   A large, long cabinet with a flat top used to support food and dishes during a meal. In some designs the cabinet is topped with a number of open shelves half or less in depth than the width of the cabinet top.

SINGLE-GATE TABLE   Table with a top that folds to one side.

SKIRT (also **APRON**)   The wood that joins the tops of two table legs together and supports the edge of the tabletop. Any horizontal piece of wood that is on edge and supports a portion of the furniture.

SLAT   A thin, flat narrow piece of wood.

SLEIGH BED   A bed shaped to somewhat resemble a sled.

SOFA   An upholstered bench with back and side arms.

SPICE CUPBOARD   A small cupboard that is usually hung on a wall.

SPINDLE   Any thin vertical portion of furniture; usually turned (made round).

SPINET   Forerunner of the harpsichord, which in turn developed into the modern piano.

SPLINT   Hickory, ash, oak, or reed split into thin strips for weaving chair backs and bottoms.

STANDARD   Any vertical support that carries a mirror, screen or similar object.

STRAP HINGE   A hinge that is long and is fastened on top of the two pieces it joins.

STRAP WORK   Furniture held together or ornamented by straps of metal, sometimes with ornamented, brass nails.

STREAKING In wood, bands or streaks of color differing from the balance of the wood. In painting, the art of using paint to make an evenly colored wood surface look as though it was heavily streaked; also to duplicate the appearance of marble on wood.

STRETCHER(S) The board or boards that join two or more furniture legs together. Also called rungs, though the term *rung* is also used to denote a horizontal piece of a chair back.

STUD An upholstery nail with a large, sometimes ornamented head.

SUITE A number of pieces of furniture preselected to serve a particular purpose and to be used together.

SWAG A swinging, hanging decoration of any kind; a strip of cloth draped over a window or door opening.

SYCAMORE A tree whose wood looks a good bit like maple. It is hard, dense, and light in color. Used mainly for carcass work as it tends to swell and warp more readily than other woods.

TALLBOY Two chests of drawers, one atop the other, the upper chest smaller than the lower, generally in depth. The two chests may or may not be separable.

TAMBOUR A shutter or door made of strips of wood or other material.

TAPESTRY Fabric woven to produce pictorial designs and normally hung on walls for decorative purposes and to keep out the chill.

TAVERN TABLE A long, low table supported by an unornamented frame. Used in America and England in taverns, approximately 1700 through 1850.

TEAK A term for a large number of Oriental trees. The wood is very dense, highly resistant to moisture and rot. It is choice timber for boats and furniture. Colors range from light to dark brown depending on the species; grain is straight and tight, and not easily split.

TÊTE-À-TÊTE A love seat in which the occupants face in opposite directions.

THONET, MICHAEL A furniture maker who perfected the method of making bentwood furniture in 1840. He was the first to mass-produce furniture successfully.

TILL   A drawer or small compartment in a table or cabinet, sometimes used to store money.

TILT-TOP TABLE   Table with its top on a hinge so that it can be lowered into a vertical position.

TONGUE AND GROOVE   A wood joint whereby a projection on the side of one board fits into a groove in the side of a second board.

TORTOISE SHELL   Pieces of the shell of the sea turtle used as inlay.

TRIPTYCH   An alterpiece with three panels.

TRIVET   Now a small, short-legged stand used for supporting hot dishes on a wood surface. Earlier, a three-legged table of metal placed near an open fire and used for warming dishes.

TRUCKLE BED   A trundle bed.

TRUMEAU   A combination of a painting and a mirror on one frame, heavily ornamented in Louis XIV and later styles.

TRUNDLE BED   A bed in two parts, the smaller of which can be slid under the larger when not in use.

TUDOR   Styles popular in England during the reigns of the Tudor kings and queens, 1485 to 1603.

TUFTING   Upholstery with ties running through it in a pattern and forming curved surfaces. Buttons on the surface hide the ties.

TULIPWOOD   Dense, heavy wood from Central America, tan with markings in red.

TURKEY   In furniture, a style featuring rounded, cushioned surfaces, in contrast to the Western style of sharp, clearly evident corners and edges.

TURNING   In woodworking, the technique of turning a piece of wood on its axis while a knife, chisel, or sandpaper is pressed against it to produce a rounded form.

VALANCE   Horizontal drapery or even wood positioned horizontally above a headboard of a bed, a window opening, or door opening.

VARNISH   A gum or similar substance, dissolved in a volatile spirit such as turpentine, that forms a hard, durable, transparent surface. Today, most varnishes used in furniture are derived chemically.

VEILLEUSE   A French chaise longue made during the period of Louis XI.

VELOUR   A kind of plush or velvet generally of wool or mohair.

VENEER   Any flat, thin material glued to the surface of any other material. In furniture, a sheet of plastic or fine wood glued to the surface of a less attractive or durable wood.

VICTORIAN   Styles and designs, common mainly to England from 1840 to 1900, during the reign of Queen Victoria, but often found in America at the same time.

VITRINE   A cabinet with clear glass doors designed for display of the objects within.

VOLUTE   A cuving spiral.

WAINSCOT   A layer of wood reaching from the floor to approximately midpoint on a wall.

WALL FURNITURE   Furniture having a flat back that permits it to be positioned against a wall.

WALNUT   A large family of trees whose wood has been greatly prized for furniture since ancient times. It is now scarce. Comes in a great variety of colors and curved grain patterns. It is hard, takes polish very well, resists moisture and rot. Natural American black walnut is gray-brown in color. In the past it was often stained to resemble ebony.

WARDROBE   Any large closet in which clothes can be hung and otherwise stored.

WARP   In wood, the tendency to twist and bend of itself upon drying or the absorption of moisture.

WASHSTAND   A small cabinet that holds a pitcher and washbasin.

WEDGEWOOD   Fine English potteryware often decorated with medallions and other cameo shapes.

WELTING   A fabric or leather edging generally turned under to produce a smooth edge.

WHAT-NOT   A tier of shelves, sometimes of varying size.

WICKER   Any natural, nonanimal fiber that may be woven. This includes grass, reeds, willows, rushes, etc. Today, some wicker is made of twisted paper.

WINDOW SEAT   A two-person bench with raised arms or sides and no back. May be upholstered.

WINDSOR   A chair style utilizing a bentwood top rail for the back frame. Developed in and around Windsor Castle sometime between 1700 and 1725.

WING   A projecting portion of a piece of furniture.

WING CHAIR   A large upholstered chair with side arms continuing up along the back.

WROUGHT IRON   Iron shaped by heating and pounding. It is flexible and tough, as contrasted to cast iron, which is brittle.

YEW   A small-bore tree furnishing red-brown wood that is hard, dense, and polishes very well. Used for furniture in ancient times and as a veneer in later times.

YUBA   Oak from Tasmania.

ZEBRAWOOD   Hard, dense wood with vivid, alternate stripes of yellow and red. Much prized as a veneer.